Mel Bay Presents

The Complete Mandolinist

A COMPREHENSIVE METHOD

by Marilynn Mair

CD Contents

1 Notes on the G string [0:35]
2 Notes on the D string [0:36]
3 Notes on the A string [0:36]
4 Notes on the E string [0:37]
5 Notes on the E and A strings [0:45]
6 Notes on the A and D strings [0:57]
7 Tremolo Duet #1 [1:02]
8 Tremolo Duet #2 [0:50]
9 Duet in G [1:30]
10 Coverdale's Carol [2:00]
11 Valse [2:20]
12 Dark Eyes [1:03]
13 A Flor Amorosa [2:27]
14 Não Se Impressione [2:00]
15 Playing Three Against Two [1:42]
16 Lyrical Duet [1:18]
17 Celeste Aida [2:12]
18 Duet in G [2:11]
19 Double Dotting [1:23]

20 Minuetto Pietoso [1:00]
21 Frequent Accidentals [1:29]
22 Shaping Music with Dynamics [1:35]
23 Habañera [1:34]
24 Minuetto Expressiovo [2:43]
25 Etude in 5/4 [1:55]
26 Invention #1 [1:27]
27 Die Zufriedenheit [1:42]
28 Komm Liebe Zither [2:11]
29 Minuet from *Don Giovanni* [2:14]
30 Iara [2:53]
31 Brejeiro [2:00]
32 East of Here [3:20]
33 Gaucho [2:07]
34 Beethoven Sonatina C minor [4:50]
35 Beethoven Sonatina C Major [2:50]
36 Vivaldi Concerto in C - 1st mvt. [2:46]
37 Vivaldi Concerto in C - 2nd mvt. [2:50]
38 Vivaldi Concerto in C - 3rd mvt. [2:08]

1 2 3 4 5 6 7 8 9 0

EXCLUSIVE SALES AGENT MEL BAY PUBLICATIONS, INC., PACIFIC, MO 63069.
INTERNATIONAL COPYRIGHT SECURED. B.M.I. MADE AND PRINTED IN U.S.A.

Visit us on the Web at www.melbay.com — E-mail us at email@melbay.com

Credits

The author would like to thank:
My teachers, especially Hibbard Perry and Vincenz Hladky, for getting me here.
My students, and Russell Foster, for pushing me to do this.
Randy Walters, for recording, editing, and mastering the book CD.
Robert Paul Sullivan, for playing the accompaniment parts on the CD.
Alexander Wohlhueter, for taking and editing the photographs in the book.
Brinsley Fair Davis, for art directing the photo session.
Joe Auger, for recording the tracks from other CDs included on the book CD.
Jacque Russom, for editing the manuscript and proofs.
Adam Larrabee, for data entry of many of the exercises.
Norman Levine and John Craton, for advice and encouragement.
My colleagues and friends, and Mel Bay for their support of this project.
Robert D. and Mary G. Mair, for nearly everything.
Brinsley Fair and Nathaniel Evans Davis, for the rest.

Marilynn Mair is a mandolinist who, through her technical mastery and artistic interpretation, has established the classical mandolin in chamber music circles worldwide. She has performed internationally for over two decades, appearing in hundreds of concerts throughout Europe, North and South America, and the Far East, including performances at Carnegie Hall, the White House, the Newport Music Festival, Lincoln Center, Tivoli Concert Hall, the Palffy Palace, the Brooklyn Academy of Music, the Palácio de Cristal and the Banff Centre for the Arts. She has represented the United States at international music festivals in Italy, France, Spain, England, Austria, Germany, Sweden, Denmark, Japan, and Brazil, earning the title "First Lady of the American Mandolin." Ms. Mair has also released several highly acclaimed CDs of mandolin music, from classical to Brazilian.

Ms. Mair began her mandolin studies with Hibbard Perry in Providence, Rhode Island, and continued them in Vienna with Professor Vincenz Hladky of the Vienna Conservatory. She also studied in Germany with mandolinist Takashi Ochi and with Siegfried Behrend, guitarist and director of the German Mandolin Orchestra. She was coached by English mandolinist Hugo d'Alton, English composer and guitarist Jack Duarte, and others, including Cuban guitarist and composer Leo Brouwer, who called her the "Angel of the tremolo." She recently studied Brazilian mandolin technique extensively with Joel Nascimento in Rio de Janeiro. As a soloist, Ms. Mair has continued to expand the parameters of mandolin technique and repertoire, and has commissioned, recorded, and performed works by many contemporary composers, including Ernst Krenek, Guido Santorsola, Evan Ziporyn, Daniel Pinkham, Ann Carr Boyd, Siegfried Behrend, David Jaffe, Will Ayton, David Hahn, Pamela Marshall, Luiz Simas, Mauricio Carrilho, and others. In addition to her solo work Ms. Mair directs the mandolin octet Enigmatica that performs Baroque, Brazilian, and contemporary music. She also performs with the New England Mandolin Ensemble, a quartet playing improvised and written music that mixes jazz, classical, and world idioms. And she is a member of Água no Feijão, a Brazilian choro group in Rio de Janeiro.

Ms. Mair is actively involved in continuing and developing the American classical mandolin tradition. She directs the American Mandolin & Guitar Summer School, a national forum for mandolin and guitar instruction held annually since 1986. In addition to her mandolin activities, Ms. Mair is a Professor of Music at Roger Williams University, in Bristol, Rhode Island, teaching music history and topics in American music and culture. Further information on Ms. Mair and music for mandolin can be found on her website: www.marilynnmair.com.

Welcome to *The Complete Mandolinist* ~

I've written this book for you, because a complete mandolinist is what I hope you'll aspire to be. The mandolin is a beautiful instrument with a long performance history in many musical styles, and to play any of them well requires a good and versatile technique. I present my path to good technique here, building on the great American mandolin methods of the early 20th century, and including exercises that go back to the 18th century. I've poured the insights of my teachers and my own quarter-century career into this project, and I intend for it to help you gain the skill and vision you'll need to become your own version of a great mandolinist.

Beyond improving your mandolin technique, I hope this book will inspire you to develop into a thinking musician. Playing with imagination and artistry is the goal of every great performer, and those instincts should be nurtured from the first lesson. I've chosen and arranged the exercises in this book to be musically satisfying, as well as technically challenging, to develop your ear and your heart along with your finger dexterity. For to be a great musician as well as a good mandolinist should be your ultimate goal.

The Complete Mandolinist is divided into five sections. "Basics" is where you'll begin if you don't play, don't read music, or suspect you might have some technical problems to solve. After that it is my intention that you work on the next four sections—*Left Hand, Right Hand, Coordination,* and *Musicianship*—at the same time, moving through each at your own speed. I hope you will enjoy this book, and that you will find your mandolin journey as interesting as I have found mine.

Composers whose works are included in this book

Bach, J. S. (1685–1750) The most famous composer of the Baroque Era.

Beethoven, L. V. (1770–1827) Classical-Era composer who wrote six pieces for mandolin and harpsichord.

Beriot, Charles de (1802–1870) Virtuoso French violinist, composer and teacher.

Bizet, Georges (1838–1875) French Romantic-Era composer, best known for his operas, especially "Carmen."

Branzoli, Giuseppe (19th century) Italian mandolinist who published "Metodo Teorico-Pratico per Mandolino" in 1875.

Calado, Joaquim (1848–1880) Brazilian flautist and early composer of choro music.

Campagnoli, Bartolomeo (1751–1827) Violinist and composer of violin studies.

Christofaro, Fernand de (19th century) Mandolinist and teacher who published his mandolin method in 1891.

Corelli, Arcangelo (1653–1713) Italian Baroque composer who introduced a more expressive style for the violin.

dall'Abaco, Evaristo (1675–1742) Italian cellist and composer.

David, Ferdinand (1810–1873) Romantic-Era German violin virtuoso and teacher.

Denis, Pietro (c. 1770) French mandolinist and teacher who published a mandolin method in three volumes.

Fiorillo, Federigo (1753–1824) Violinist and composer.

Foster, Stephen (1826–1864) American composer of lovely and quintessentially nationalistic ballads.

Fouchetti, Giovanni (c. 1770) Italian mandolinist and teacher who published a method for mandolin.

Gonzaga, Chiquinha (1847–1945) Pianist, composer, activist, and one of the originators of Brazilian choro.

Kayser, Henry (1815–1888) German composer of studies for violin and viola.

Kreutzer, Rudolf (1766–1831) Classical violinist and teacher.

LeClair, Jean (1697–1764) French violinist and composer.

Leone, Gabriele (1725–1790) French Classical-Era mandolinist who published a method for mandolin in 1768.

MacDowell, Edward (1861–1908) American Impressionist composer.

Mazas, Jacques (1782–1849) French violinist and composer.

Medeiros, Anacleto de (1866–1907) A bandleader, and one of the earliest composers of Brazilian choro music.

Meerts, Lambert (1800–1863) Belgian violinist and teacher.

Mozart, Leopold (1719–1787) Austrian violinist and teacher, father of Wolfgang.

Mozart, Wolfgang Amadeus (1756–1791) Classical composer who wrote two songs and an aria accompanied by mandolin.

Nazareth, Ernesto (1863–1934) Pianist, composer, and one of the originators of Brazilian choro music.

O'Carolan, Turlough (1630–1738) Blind Irish harpist and composer of beloved instrumental tunes.

Odell, Herbert Forrest (1872–1926) Mandolinist and teacher from Boston, Massachusetts, who published his multi-volume "Method for the Mandolin" in 1906.

Pettine, Giuseppe (1874–1966) Italian mandolinist and teacher from Providence, Rhode Island, who published his 7-volume "Modern Mandolin School" from 1901–1906.

Pleyel, Ignaz Josef (1757–1831) Viennese violinist, composer, and student of Haydn.

Ranieri, Silvio (c. 1900) Mandolin virtuoso whose method, "L'Art de Mandoline" was published in 1910.

Schloming, Harry (c. 1850) Composer of violin studies published in the Seybold methods in 1915.

Seybold, Arthur (1868–1948) Violinist and teacher who published his violin method in 12 volumes in 1915.

Siegel, Samuel (1875–1948) American mandolinist known for duo-style. He published "Special Mandolin Studies" in 1901.

Spohr, Louis (1784–1859) violin virtuoso and teacher.

Sponer, Alfred von (c. 1900) Composer of violin studies, published in Seybold methods in 1915.

Verdi, Giuseppe (1813–1901) Famous Italian opera composer of the Romantic Era.

Wichtl, Georg (1805–1877) Violinist and teacher.

Wohlfahrt, Franz (1833–1884) Composer of a famous series of studies for the violin.

Composers of American mandolin methods whose work is not included in this book for copyright and other reasons:

Abt, Valentine (1873–1942) Published a mandolin method in three volumes in 1902, based on Kayser's violin studies.

Bickford, Zahr Myron (1876–1960) Published a famous mandolin method in four volumes c. 1920.

Place, William (1889–1959) Published his three-volume method in 1934. I began my mandolin studies with Hibbard Perry using this method.

Table of Contents

*recorded on the book CD

Table of Contents

*recorded on the book CD

Holding the Mandolin

When you begin to play the mandolin, it's best to start in a seated position without using a strap. Sit up straight with both feet on the floor and your shoulders relaxed. Hold the mandolin on your right thigh with the instrument's head at about shoulder level and the top of the instrument facing straight ahead, not angled to the right. Be sure your chair allows your feet to rest flat on the floor and your mandolin to rest securely on your leg.

The mandolin neck should rest on the side of your left-hand index finger well behind the first knuckle, and your thumb should rest lightly on the top side of the neck at about the 2nd or 3rd fret. The knuckles at the base of your fingers should be even with the edge of the fretboard, not below it. Make sure your shoulders are level and your arms fall easily from the shoulders; don't hold your elbows out from the body in a tense position. Be sure you can easily flop all four fingers in unison up and down on each of the four strings. If you have trouble reaching any strings or frets, check the previous information again and readjust your hand position.

 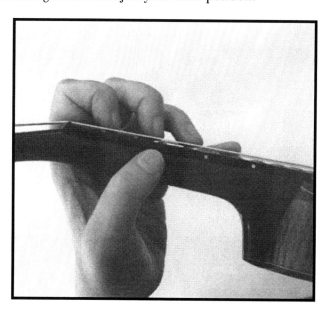

While it is possible to elevate your right leg using a footstool or crossing your legs, or hold the head of the mandolin up using a strap, it's better to begin your study sitting in the simplest and most natural posture to avoid unnecessary strain on your body.

Choosing a Pick

You should use a small heavy pick with a precise point to play the mandolin. The most easily available are the small heavy guitar picks by Gibson, Martin, or Peavey, although if you can find the out-of-production small heavy Pettine picks or a fairly thick real or imitation tortoise-shell pick you'll be pleased by their tone. The strings on the mandolin are high-tension, which is why you need to use a heavy pick in order to move them. When choosing a pick, be sure that it has a solid feel but retains some flexibility. Large thin guitar picks won't work well, but neither will very thick unbendable jazz guitar picks. Your goal is to have a pick that is heavy enough to move your strings with enough force to set the body of your instrument in motion (because the body of your instrument gives the note its tone color), while retaining enough flexibility so the pick can give slightly on contact with the string to soften impact. A large thin guitar pick will bend too much on contact and create a lot of noise when you pick (think of a playing card in bicycle spokes), and it won't move the strings sufficiently to get the best tone from your instrument. An unbendable guitar pick will hit the strings too hard, and won't give you the blend needed to create a good tremolo from rapid down-up strokes. A narrow contact point on your pick will give you a more focused sound, also important to developing a clear expressive tremolo. Resist the temptation to play with a rounded-off point on your pick. Yes, in the short term it will keep your pick from getting caught in the strings, and it will give a dark mellow sound. But without a point you are permanently removing bright tone color from your musical vocabulary by muting the overtones. A pointed pick will ultimately give you a much broader range of tone color as you develop your right-hand technique to create sounds from bright to dark. Your pick creates your musical persona, so choose wisely. Here are some examples of several picks that will work well, and four that won't.

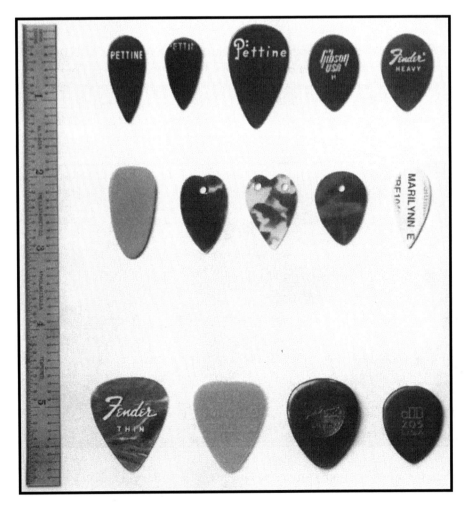

BEST: Top row left to right:
(These are the picks I use)
Small heavy Pettine pick.
A cut-down Pettine pick I often use.
Large heavy Pettine, still available, good for mandola & mandocello.
Gibson small heavy guitar pick.
Fender small heavy guitar pick.

GOOD: 2nd row left to right:
(These are picks used by friends)
Green .88 Dunlop Tortex, originally standard size, but cut narrower.
Japanese tortoise-shell pick.
Japanese plastic pick.
Brazilian small heavy plastic pick.
Example of a pick cut from an ID card to the small Pettine specs.

DON'T USE: 3rd row:
(two are too thin; two are too thick)
Fender standard thin guitar pick.
Thin Brazilian pick that comes inside some packs of bandolim strings. Dunlop Big Stubby Flatpick.
Dunlop Jazztone 205.

Holding the Pick

Hold your right arm out in front of you with a straight elbow, relax your hand and let it drop. Curl your fingers in toward the palm, stopping about an inch before they get there. Swing your thumb in to meet the side of the first joint of the index finger, keeping your hand relaxed. Maintain that hand position and bring your hand down to playing position. Insert your pick between the ball of your thumb and the side of your index finger, perpendicular to your thumb and nearly perpendicular to the first digit of your index finger. Be sure to keep your hand relaxed. Hold your right hand so you can't see any of the knuckles of your hand beyond the first one. Maintain an open "half-circle" relationship between the thumb and index finger and don't grip your pick so tightly that it can't move a little on contact with the string. You should have a slight arch to your right wrist, and your right arm should fall easily from the shoulder. When you drop your hand to play through the string, drop it from the wrist, not the elbow, so your forearm rotates slightly. Return your hand to its original position with a simple lift motion. Now you're ready to begin. The flat of your pick should contact the string; don't play using the side or the edge of the pick. At the same time your pick should be slightly oblique to the string, as you can see in the last picture. This allows the weight of your hand to pull the pick easily down through the string. Play your open strings now with down-strokes, using a "rest stroke" so that the pick carries right through the pair of strings you are playing to rest firmly against the top string of the next pair. While you will not always play with a rest stroke, using it in the beginning reinforces correct right-hand position, and insures that you are playing both strings in the pair with your down-stroke. It should also keep you playing with an easy "drop-lift" and prevent you from adopting a "push-pull" pick technique that causes more tension in the wrist and hinders development of a smooth tremolo. And it will prevent you from wasting effort by picking uselessly up into the air after your pick leaves the string.

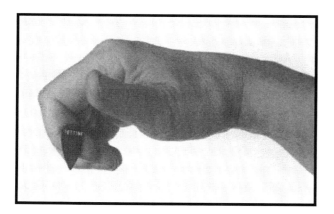
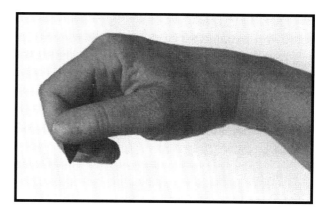

Developing Your Sound

The quality of sound you produce as you play the mandolin is an important element in establishing your musical persona. It is the first thing people notice about your playing and strongly affects how they perceive your music. Just as your speaking or singing voice colors your words, your tone color transmits your notes to an audience, and can enhance or detract from your performance immeasurably. Fast picking can impress, but only if it is delivered with a true sound and, ideally, the variety of a broad sound palette. The instrument you play, the pick and strings you use, and your right- and left-hand technique all contribute to creating your individual voice on the mandolin. As you progress through this book, you will feel a sense of accomplishment as you begin to play cleaner, faster, and feel more at home on your instrument. At the same time you are working on technique, however, you should also be developing your ear, so you can begin to define your personal sound as a mandolinist. Tone color and quality of sound are powerful tools that you can use as you begin to play more expressively.

You should pay attention to the quality of sound you produce on your instrument from the very first exercises you play. For that reason the first pieces on the book CD are the first duets in the book. Take time to "play with" your instrument as well as studying it, and explore the variety of sounds you can produce for a single note. Then as your technical expertise develops you'll also be accumulating a vocabulary of sound you can begin to apply for expressive purposes. Play each open string in all possible locations, from right behind the bridge, which gives a harsh metallic sound, to well over the fingerboard, which is the mandolin's "dolce" region. Take note of all the different sounds you can produce—you may need to employ each of them one day. These are just some of the questions a thinking musician needs to consider in the process of creating a musical performance.

Figuring out how to play the written notes in an exercise or a concert piece is just the beginning of the process of making music. To play musically you need to consider all sides of each note—the quality of attack you use to begin it, how you choose to sustain it, when and how you choose to end it, and if and how you connect it to other notes in a phrase. Do you want your note to end abruptly to create a staccato sound, or connect seamlessly with the next note to make a legato phrase? What dynamic level do you want to play, and how will each note fit into the pattern of dynamics you are creating? Does the tremolo fit your interpretation of a particular piece, and if so how will you use it? If not, how will you sustain and connect long notes? These are just some of the questions a thinking mandolinist needs to consider to create a musical performance.

Please don't be daunted by this list of musical objectives, especially if you are just beginning to play. The most graceful ballerina was once a child learning to walk, and you need to give yourself time to learn how to get fingers to frets. But I am suggesting that after you get your metaphorical feet under you, you begin to pay attention to the sound you produce on your mandolin. It has the potential to be one of the most personal and satisfying things you will ever create in your lifetime. Learn to develop and enjoy your unique personality as a mandolinist. Yes, you'll have mando-heroes you learn from, but, eventually, you should strive to become unique as a player. You have the power to play as beautifully, coolly, strongly, or sharply as you wish, and hopefully all of those by turn, as it suits the variety of music you choose to play. Don't underestimate the power of your right-hand technique to bring music to life. Armed with only a small piece of plastic you can create a world of incredible tone color if you learn to hear and desire it, and develop the musical intelligence needed to create it.

Mandolin Basics

Reading Music on the Mandolin

Reading music is a straightforward business, and we can simplify it even more by focusing on reading music for the mandolin. Many mandolinists don't read music, and play "by ear" (copying what they hear others play) or use tablature, an alternate notation system used to write out American folk music on fretted string instruments. Learning to read music puts a whole world of musical styles at your fingertips and is an important skill for becoming a complete mandolinist. Here are the 7 basic elements we'll be working with:

1. **Staff** - The Staff is a set of 5 lines. On, between, above, and below these lines musical notes are written. Every line and space has a particular name, and we'll be learning these as they relate to the names of the open strings and the fretted notes on the mandolin.

2. **Treble Clef** - Music for mandolin is written in the Treble Clef. Other instruments, like the violin and flute, also use Treble Clef. Some instruments use other clefs, like the the Bass or the Tenor, and the piano uses two clefs at once. The mandolin just uses Treble, so that's all you need to know about clefs.

3. **Key Signature** - We'll learn more about these later. Basically, the Key Signature identifies which musical scale a particular piece will use. Sharps or flats are used to indicate which scale, or key, a piece is written in. For instance, the Key Signature in our example, two sharps, indicates the Key of D. We'll begin our study with the Key of C, no sharps or flats, so you don't have to worry about Key Signatures yet.

4. **Time Signature** - The Time Signature is made up of two numbers, set up like a fraction. The bottom number gives you the unit of measurement (quarter notes, eighth notes, etc.) and the top number indicates how many of these units will be in a bar, or measure, of music. Our example is written in "three-four," or "three-quarter" time. A quarter note gets a beat and there are 3 beats in each measure.

5. **Notes** - A note has a head and a stem. The head appears on the staff in a place that indicates, for our purposes, the fret and the string of the mandolin that will be played. This is where we'll do most of our early reading work, learning where all the written notes are found on the fretboard, and how to combine notes to produce a tune. Different types of note heads and stems are used to indicate how long a note lasts. In our example, measure 1 uses "quarter notes" that, according to our time signature, get one beat each. Measure 2 has two quarter notes, and two "eighth notes," that get a half-beat each. Measure 3 uses a "half note" that gets two beats, and two eighth notes. The "dotted half note" in measure 5 gets three beats. You'll learn more about how to identify the length of each note as you move through the book.

6. **Bar Lines** - These are the vertical lines written across the staff to divide a piece of music into equal measures. The particular unit for each piece is determined by its Time Signature. In our example, the Time Signature of "three-four" indicates that there will be a bar line every three beats.

7. **Rests** - Rests are used in music to indicate a spot where no notes are played. Measure 4, above, begins with a "quarter-note rest" indicating that nothing is to be played on the first beat. Like notes, rests have different values, and we'll learn more about these as we move ahead.

Open Strings / Notes in First Position

Pick each open string easily, using a down-stroke (the symbol for down-stroke appears over the first four notes of this exercise). Be sure to maintain a slightly arched, relaxed wrist, and pick downward through the string until your pick rests on the next string. Count the beats in each measure, and maintain an even tempo. When you place your left-hand fingers on the strings, be sure to place them just behind the fret, to prevent buzzes. Keep fingers down as long as possible to make it easier for the next higher finger to press the string to the fret. The double-dot symbol used at the end of each section of music indicates that you should repeat that section before proceeding to the next section.

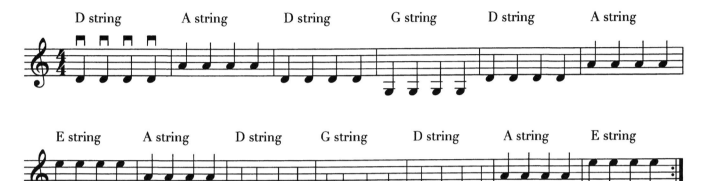

Notes on the D String

Notes on the D String - Play each note with a down-stroke. Repeat each section as indicated. Your 1st finger is on the 2nd fret; 2nd finger on the 3rd fret; and 3rd finger on the 5th fret.

Notes on the A String

Notes on the A String - Play each note with a down-stroke. Repeat each section as indicated. Your 1st finger is on the 2nd fret; 2nd finger on the 3rd fret; and 3rd finger on the 5th fret, just like the D string.

Notes on the E String

Notes on the E String - Play each note with a down-stroke. Repeat each section as indicated. Your 1st finger is on the 1st fret; 2nd finger on the 3rd fret; 3rd finger on the 5th fret; 4th finger on the 7th fret.

Notes on the G String

Notes on the G String - Play each note with a down-stroke. Repeat each section as indicated. Your 1st finger is on the 2nd fret; 2nd finger on the 4th fret; and 3rd finger on the 5th fret.

13

First Duets

Play all the notes with down-strokes and be sure to hold each note for its proper length. You do this by keeping your finger down on the string until it's time for the next note to be played. Notes on the 7th fret have been added for all strings, and these are to be played with the 4th finger. The note at the 7th fret is exactly the same pitch as the next higher open string. Count evenly and listen to the accompaniment part so you don't speed up or cut a note short. Observe the repeat marks at the end of each exercise.

Notes on the E String - Mair  Tr. 4

Notes on the E and A Strings - Odell Tr. 5

Notes on the A and D Strings - Pettine

The ♯ sign, used in Measure 8, indicates that a note is "sharp" and is to be played a fret higher than usual. When a sharp is used in a measure it remains in effect for the rest of that measure but returns to its "natural" state when the bar line is crossed. The accompaniment part in this duet includes notes on the D and G Strings. It should be played by the teacher at first, but later may be played by the student. Use the 4th finger where indicated.

 Tr. 6

16

Adding the Up-stroke

As you add up-strokes (see symbol in measure 1) in these exercises, be sure not to change your right hand position. Play your down-stroke quarter notes thinking about the silent up-stroke you are making between them. When you add the up-stroke on the eighth notes, play it lightly, only hitting one string of the pair. Always keep your wrist relaxed and keep the beat steady.

Rosina Mazurka - Pettine

Play the quarter notes down-stroke and the eighth notes down-up. "D. C. al Fine" (Da Capo — "from the head," al Fine — "to the end") indicates that the player should go back to the beginning of the piece and play until reaching the "Fine" marking in the music.

Three Tunes

It's important—and fun—to play songs as well as exercises. Tunes have a natural flow, and you'll begin to develop your musical ear. Here are some folk tunes for you to try. You can add a little swing to the notes or vary the melody—it's an accepted part of the folk tradition. Chords are indicated for teacher accompaniment now, and for your enjoyment later. They can be played on guitar or on another mandolin. Charts of the many varieties of chord fingerings are not included in this book, because of space, but there are many readily available in print or online. Count evenly, giving the notes their full value, and hold the long notes for their full duration. The quarter-note rests used in the first piece are to be given one beat each.

Acres of Clams

Black Jack Davy

Nonesuch

Developing Coordination & Reading Skills

These exercises include notes of different values. The quarter note gets one beat, so the eighth note gets a half beat, the sixteenth note gets a quarter beat, and the dotted quarter note gets one-and-a-half beats. Play the dotted quarter note with a down-stroke and the eighth note that follows it with an up-stroke, except when marked differently. Pairs of eighth notes are played down-up. A time signature of "C" appears for the first time in these pieces. "C" stands for "Common Time" and is frequently used in place of a 4/4 time signature. An F♯ appears part-way through this exercise. Remember that the "sharp" in front of the note indicates that the note is to be played a fret higher than the "natural" unaltered note.

D, A, and E strings - Wichtl

Locating notes - Use these arpeggios to test your quick note recall on all four strings. An "arpeggio" is a series of notes that belong to a chord, but are written and played sequentially.

A, D, and G strings - de Beriot Keep your left-hand fingers down as long as possible for a legato feel.

Mazurka on the Fourth String - Pettine This exercise uses notes on the G string and includes rests.

Melody in C - Christofaro Here is another arpeggio-based exercise to check your quick note recall.

Notes on all 4 strings - de Beriot Be sure to use your 4th finger where indicated in this exercise. An F♯ is used in this exercise, along with an F♮. A "natural" sign indicates that the note returns to its normal position. The F♮ in this piece is a "courtesy accidental." It's not really necessary, because you've crossed a bar line so the F♯ is no longer in effect, but it's written anyway as a reminder.

Down-Up Picking - Spohr Play the sixteenth notes down-up and the eighth notes with down-strokes.

21

Preparing to Tremolo

One of the most recognizable features of good mandolin technique is a smooth, expressive tremolo. Like the bowing of an accomplished violinist, tremolo allows the player to lengthen a note and, through judicious application, create an interpretive phrase. Tremolo is not essential to phrasing, and a great tremolo can't make up for lack of musicianship. But in the hands of an artistic performer, tremolo is an unparalleled vehicle to communicate emotion through sound.

Developing good tremolo technique is a slow and sometimes frustrating process that few can shortcut. But once mastered, a smooth tremolo is yours for life. Tremolo is created from a series of rapid down- and up-strokes, so you need to start the process with a good right-hand foundation. Assess your regular picking style to insure that you've achieved an ease and flexibility that will allow you to progress. Begin your diagnostic check by picking down-up slowly and regularly on your open D or A string. Is your wrist relaxed? Is your forearm relaxed? Is your picking even? As your pick moves the string, does the string also move your pick? Are you picking down through both strings of the pair, but up on only one? Can you continue to pick this way for a couple of minutes without a change in arm tension or sound? Can you play without placing your right-hand pinkie on the face of the mandolin? (Dragging it is OK; anchoring it is not.) If the answer to each of these questions is "yes," then you are ready to proceed.

As you prepare to tremolo be sure your right-hand pinkie is relaxed and just brushes the face of the mandolin. You should use a small heavy pick (or a large pick with a sharp point) and hold it lightly so it moves between your fingers as it strikes the strings. On the down-stroke let the pick come to rest on the next pair of strings before beginning the up-stroke. Don't change your hand position at all between the down- and up-strokes, simply drop and lift your hand from the wrist (not the elbow).

As you play "Exercise 1" on the next page notice if the evenness of your picking starts to break down. If so, you've probably begun too fast, so start again at a slower pace. As you proceed through the exercise you'll probably feel your wrist tighten slightly by the last measure, which is normal. Each time you repeat the exercise use the first measure of quarter notes to consciously relax your wrist before you build up the picking speed again. Optimally you should be able to repeat the exercise 10-20 times without stopping, but in no case should you continue to the point of pain. Remember, at this stage you're only responsible for maintaining relaxation and steady regular picking; speed will come later.

If you're having difficulty after working on this for a few days you may need to consider changing your wrist position to allow for easier movement. Relaxation is crucial to develop the speed and control needed for a good tremolo, and any unnecessary tension will stand between you and your goal. Check your wrist for evidence of tension. Does it rotate freely as you pick? Is your down-up picking pattern accomplished with a "drop-lift" motion rather than a "push-pull"? (This lessens wrist tension.) If not, try slightly arching your wrist to encourage freer mobility. Remember, relaxation with control is the key.

As you play your tremolo exercises, listen to be sure that your down-stroke sounds slightly louder than your up-stroke. If that's not the case, relax your hand even more on the up-stroke to soften the pick's initial attack. Although it may appear counterintuitive, a softer up-stroke will actually make your tremolo seem more even and natural, as it imitates the iambic cadence of speech, giving the sound of the rapid repetition of notes a better flow.

Tremolo Exercises

Be sure to keep your right hand relaxed and your stroke continuous on these exercises. Use a metronome to keep your picking even. Don't go too quickly at first—an even stroke is much more important at this stage than speed. Speed will come later. Your hand position should remain the same as the one you have used for down- and up-strokes, and you should play with a metronome speed of quarter note = 60 or less to start.

Exercise 1 - Repeat this exercise several times on each string, using a metronome to keep an even pulse.

Exercise 2 - Branzoli   Play each quarter note as four sixteenth notes. The first measures are written out, and you should continue that picking throughout. Count every beat and play the sixteenth notes lightly. Don't break your even sixteenth-note picking within a slurred phrase. Notice how the slurs divide the notes into groups and try to hear each group as a unit.

continue to play sixteenth-notes throughout the piece

Exercise 3 - Continue to develop your tremolo by increasing the density of your notes.

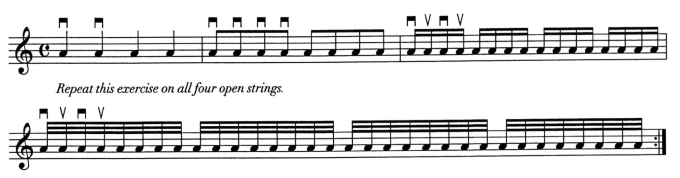

Repeat this exercise on all four open strings.

Exercise 4 - Wichtl Play these notes with a fixed-speed tremolo. Use 8 pairs of down-up strokes for each half note. Keep your tremolo steady within slurred phrases and break it slightly between phrases. The length of the phrases I've marked may seem arbitrary at first, but it's important to realize that the bar line does not necessarily indicate a break in a phrase. Combining notes in longer phrases and phrasing over the bar line are effective interpretive tools you'll need in future, so it's important for you to begin to hear the possibilities of a variety of phrasing options from the start so you will choose wisely when the decision is left to you.

Tremolo Duets

You should learn both parts of these duets. Tremolo the notes under each slur without a break, and be sure to tremolo for the full value of the last note in each phrase. Break your tremolo briefly between slurred phrases to allow the music to breathe, but don't lose the beat. Continuing to count while playing tremolo is crucial. You should always know exactly when one note ends and the next begins to keep your playing clean.

Duet 1 - Odell Tr. 7

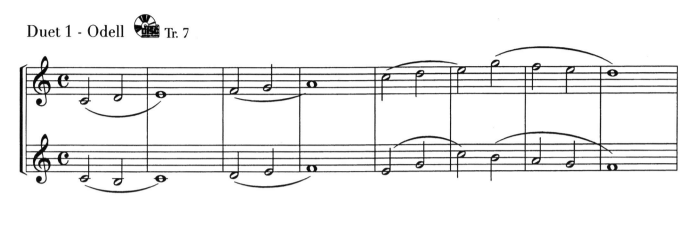

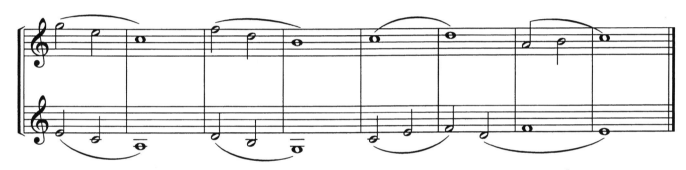

Duet 2 - Odell This exercise uses an accidental, B♭, in the lower part. B♭ is played on the 1st fret of the A string and the 3rd fret of the G string, a fret lower than a B note.

Tr. 8

Adding Accidentals

An "accidental" is a sharp or flat added to a particular note that is not part of the original key signature of the piece. The accidentals of F♯ and B♭ are used in this piece. An accidental stays in effect for the rest of the measure it appears in, but doesn't travel over the bar line to the next measure. Since this can be confusing a natural sign is often added to the note in the measure after an accidental is used, though it's not required, to remind the player that the accidental is now no longer in effect. This is called a "courtesy accidental."

Exercise - Leopold Mozart (Wolfgang's dad)

Counting & Tremolo

When you tremolo it's important to keep the "big beat" in mind so you play your notes in time. The fact that you are now playing a note with many pick strokes doesn't alter the fact that the first down-stroke of each tremolo note must be played on the beat. Practice that in these exercises. Tremolo all notes under the slur markings, and take the piece slowly enough that you can tremolo at least in 32nd notes (that's eight strokes for each quarter note). "D. C. al Fine" tells you to go back to the start of the piece and play until you reach the "Fine". In measures 13 and 14, the triple slashes across the note stems indicate that the notes are to be tremoloed, but not phrased together.

Duet 1 - W. J. Smith

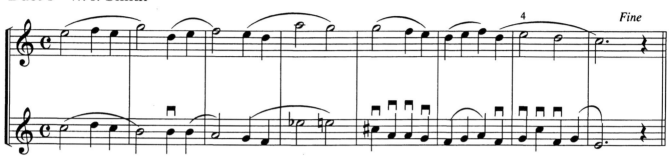

The Major Scales

Major scales all follow the same pattern, using the same series of whole steps (2-fret distance) and half steps (1-fret distance) no matter what note they start on. When you begin a major scale on C, the notes of the scale are the "natural" notes, with naturally occurring half steps between notes 3 and 4, and notes 7 and 8, and all other notes separated by a whole step. When you begin a major scale on another note, sharps or flats are added to some notes to preserve the scale pattern. Since these notes will always be sharp or flat in the scale, they are designated at the beginning of the piece in a "key signature." Unlike "accidentals," sharps or flats in the key signature apply in the whole piece. Here are some one-octave major scales in a variety of keys.

C Major Scale

G Major Scale You can see from the key signature that the F note is always sharp in this scale.

D Major Scale The F and C notes are always sharp in this scale.

A Major Scale

E Major Scale

F Major Scale The B note is always flat in this scale.

B♭ Major Scale

E♭ Major Scale

A♭ Major Scale

Key of G Major

The "key signature" of a piece shows the sharps or flats that will be in effect for the entire piece. The key of G Major has one sharp, F♯, that is used throughout. G Major is a popular key for writing fiddle tunes and folk music and works well for mandolin, as the "tonic" note (name note of the scale) is the lowest string,

G Major scale

Exercise in G - Branzoli
Notice how the 4th beat of each measure leads to the 1st beat of the next measure. This is a device composers frequently use to keep the momentum of a piece moving forward. Notice too that slurs are not always used to indicate tremolo; sometimes they simply indicate phrasing.

Old Molly Hare
The dotted eighth note used in this piece is equal in time value to three sixteenth notes. Play the tune with a light cheerful bounce, but be sure to give the dotted eighths their full value.

Tunes in New Keys

Try out two of your new keys in these tunes. Remember that sharps and flats in the key signature apply to all notes in the piece. Accidentals, notes written in the music that differ from the key signature, apply just in the measure where they are written.

Angelina Baker - The dotted quarter notes in this piece are equal in time value to three eighth notes. The whole note, first found in measure 4, gets four beats, a whole measure. Play the pairs of eighth notes down-up and the eighth note that follows the dotted quarter note with an up-stroke.

Archie Menzie's Reel - The key of F is unusual for a fiddle tune, so be sure to remember your B♭. In this tune you have several long runs of sixteenth notes that will give you a chance to improve the coordination between your right and left hand.

A Look at Positions

Up to this point, all of the music you have played has been in 1st position. You may have noticed that you are only using half of your fingerboard. This will change when you begin to play in positions. On the A-string you ordinarily begin with your 1st finger on B which puts you in 1st position. And in 1st position you ordinarily would play the C with your 2nd finger. If, instead, you begin to play on the A-string with your first finger on C, then you are playing in 2nd position. And if you start with your 1st finger on D, the note played by your 3rd finger in 1st position, then you are playing in 3rd position. Here are a few exercises to get you used to the concept of playing up the neck. We'll do more position work later in the method.

Exercise 1 - In this exercise you'll move up and down the neck one position at a time, playing notes on the D and A strings.

Exercise 2 - Here you'll play the notes of the C Major scale in two different places on the fretboard.

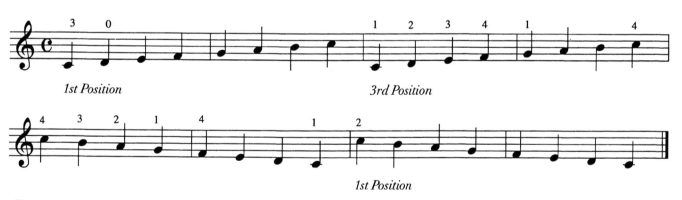

Exercise 3 - This exercise is the same as Exercise 2, but written in the key of G Major.

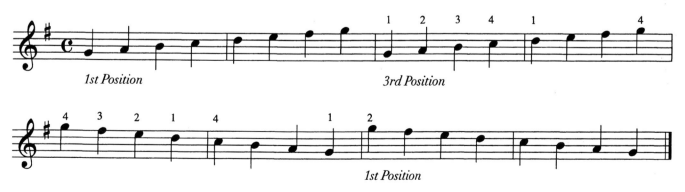

31

Duet in C

Giuseppe Branzoli (arr. Mair)

You have now finished the "Basics" section of the book and are ready to start working in the next 4 sections of *The Complete Mandolinist*. Congratulations! Here's a duet to celebrate your promotion. Tremolo under slurs and as marked, and be sure to follow the dynamic markings given. In measures 3 and 4 you'll see your first "crescendo" and "decrescendo" markings. These symbols indicate that a phrase should gradually get louder or softer. Follow all written dynamic markings to create an expressive interpretation of this duet.

Tr. 9

The Left Hand

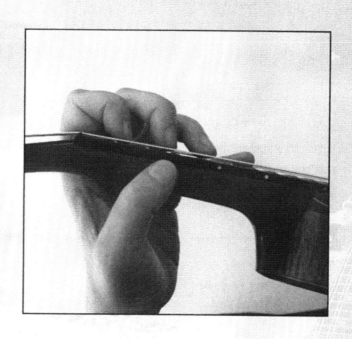

Left-Hand Technique

Your left hand is the one that finds the notes on the fingerboard, and you need to learn to do that with precision, ease, and speed. Scales and arpeggios are a good place to start to perfect correct finger placement, so we will begin there. Our first set of scale and arpeggio exercises are in 1st position, but you will eventually learn to play in all keys on the extent of the usable mandolin fingerboard. It might not sound like creative work, but it's an essential component to develop the flexible technique you need to become a more versatile musician.

The mandolin uses diatonic fingering, so each left-hand finger is responsible for covering two or three frets. This is different from the guitar; that's played with chromatic fingering using one finger for each fret. On the mandolin, your left-hand fingers are constantly required to readjust depending on which fret they are asked to play. You have to make the choice quickly and accurately so you won't play the wrong note, cause the note to buzz, or otherwise interfere with the music you're attempting to perform. In first position your first finger plays the 1st and 2nd frets, and your second finger plays the 3rd and 4th frets. Your third finger plays the 5th fret, and sometimes the 4th or 6th. Your fourth finger plays the 6th or 7th fret, sometimes the 8th. What fret your finger will play depends on the scale itself. Follow the fingering given in these scale and arpeggio exercises so your fingers will get used to adjusting their position on the fretboard accurately.

Major scales all follow a set pattern of notes separated by a series of half steps (1 fret) and whole steps (2 frets). The C Major scale uses the natural, letter-name notes, C-D-E-F-G-A-B-C. This gives us a template for the Major scale pattern: whole-whole-half-whole-whole-whole-half. To preserve this pattern in other keys, sharps or flats are added to certain scale notes and those sharps and flats become part of the key signature of the scale. Each Major scale has a "relative minor" scale that shares its key signature, but begins a third lower. Minor scales vary in their up and down patterns for melody instruments by raising the 6th and 7th tones a half step on the ascending scale and returning the notes to their usual positions for the descending scale. You don't have to remember to raise these notes by yourself, an "accidental" (a sharp, flat, or natural written before a particular note that changes its pitch from the one set by the key signature) is added before each raised note in the melodic minor scales.

Arpeggios are broken chords, and the arpeggio exercises in this section are based on the chord made up of the 1st, 3rd, and 5th notes of the scale, the tonic triad. Playing arpeggios helps you learn your fingerboard by leaps as well as steps, and improves your hand coordination. Be sure to play your arpeggios slowly and accurately, both up and down. Don't hunt for the notes as this confuses your motor memory and keeps it from learning the correct finger placement. After each pair of Major/minor scales and arpeggios, you'll find a series of exercises written in those keys. These exercises further develop your ability to play in a particular key. Follow the picking patterns indicated in each exercise and hold your left-hand fingers down as long as possible to create a legato feel. Try to play all of the notes cleanly, adjusting your fingers between frets as required. You can slowly increase your playing speed as you practice, as long as you maintain a clear tone and precise fingering. Be sure to learn all of the keys in this section. You may just be playing in C and G now, but you never know what keys your future world of music will be written in, and you'll want to be prepared.

C Major: Scales & Arpeggios

The C-Major scale uses the natural notes, and so its key signature has no sharps or flats. Play these exercises in 1st position, using the 4th finger where indicated, and extending the 4th finger to reach the high C note, on the 8th fret of the E string. The C-Major arpeggio uses the notes of the C-Major chord: C, E, and G.

2-octave C-Major scale

2-octave C-Major arpeggio

Exercise in C Major - Play this exercise using down-up picking.

A minor: Scales & Arpeggios

The key of A minor shares the same key signature as C Major, and is called its "relative minor." This exercise uses the "melodic minor" version of the scale; that version raises the 6th and 7th notes leading up to the tonic using accidentals, but returns to the regular scale notes on the way down. Sharps appear in front of F and G on the ascending scale, and "courtesy accidental" natural signs are added in the descending scale, to remind you that the notes have returned to their normal positions.

2-octave A-minor scale

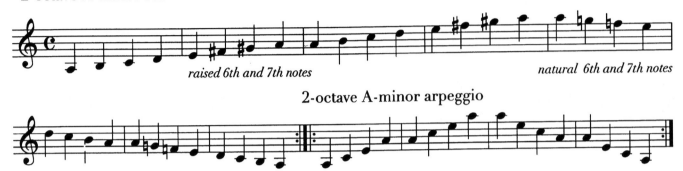

raised 6th and 7th notes　　　　　　　　　　　　　　　　*natural 6th and 7th notes*

2-octave A-minor arpeggio

Exercise in A minor - You'll notice that the F and G are only sharped in the ascending passages where they actually lead to the tonic note. Otherwise they remain in their natural state.

Exercises in C Major & A minor

Here are three exercises by different composers that modulate between the keys of C Major and A minor. You may need to tackle just half of the exercise at a time until you build up your left-hand endurance, but soon you should be able to play each exercise 2 or 3 times in a row. Use down-up picking throughout.

Exercise 1 - Wichtl

Exercise 2 - Branzoli This exercise combines scale and arpeggio passages and gives your left hand a good workout on every string. Be sure to use the 4th finger where indicated, and note that you actually shift into 2nd position briefly in measure 63.

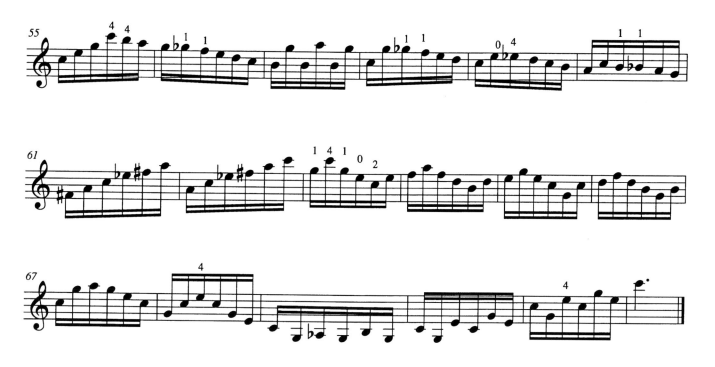

Exercise 3 - Seybold This exercise includes a variety of passages to develop your hand coordination and get your fingers used to changing their fret placement frequently, as is often necessary in minor keys.

Arpeggio Exercise in A minor

Fiorillo - This arpeggio exercise uses the notes from several different chords in the key of A minor. Play all eighth and dotted eighth notes down-stroke and sixteenth notes up-stroke. The ornaments in measures 24 and 27 are to be played with a quick down-up before the first beat of measures 24 and 27.

G Major: Scales & Arpeggios

The key signature for G Major has one sharp. When a sharp is placed in the key signature, it indicates that the note is sharped for the entire piece, unless it's altered with an accidental. Use the 4th finger where indicated.

2-octave G-Major scale

2-octave G-Major arpeggio

Exercise in G Major

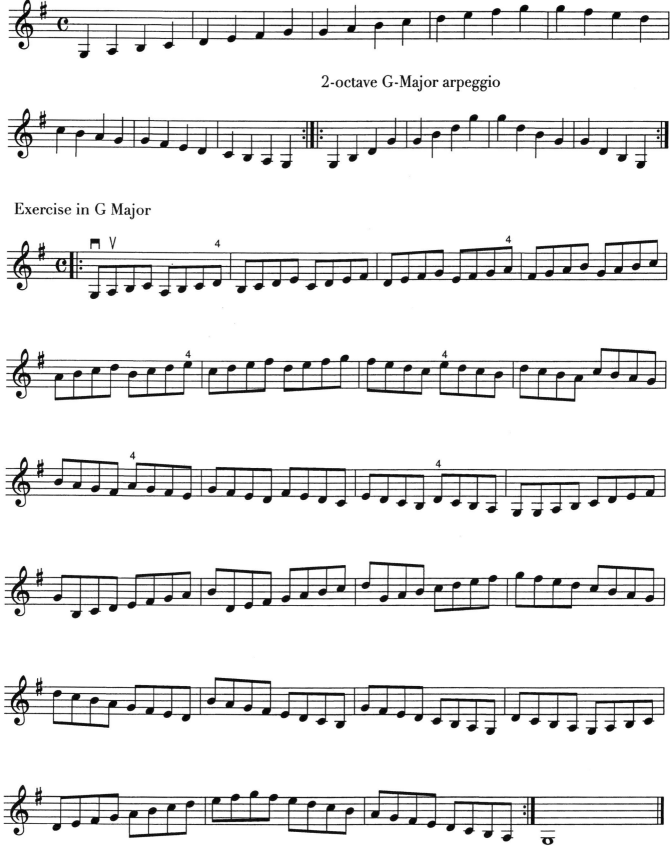

E minor: Scales & Arpeggios

E minor is the relative minor to G Major and they share the same key signature. The melodic minor scale raises the 6th and 7th tones leading up to the tonic, so C♯ and D♯ are used as accidentals going up and return to naturals going down. Note that you use your 4th finger to play the C♯ on the G-string to make it easier to reach the D♯ on the next string with your 1st finger.

1-octave E-minor scale

2-octave E-minor arpeggio

Exercise in E minor

Exercises in G Major & E minor

Exercise in G Major - de Beriot

Exercise in E minor - Odell

43

Dexterity Exercise in G Major - Wohlfahrt

44

D Major: Scales & Arpeggios

The key signature for D Major has 2 sharps, F♯ and C♯. Use the 4th finger where indicated, and keep your fingers down on ascending passages for a legato feel.

1-octave D-Major scale

2-octave D-Major arpeggio

Exercise in D Major

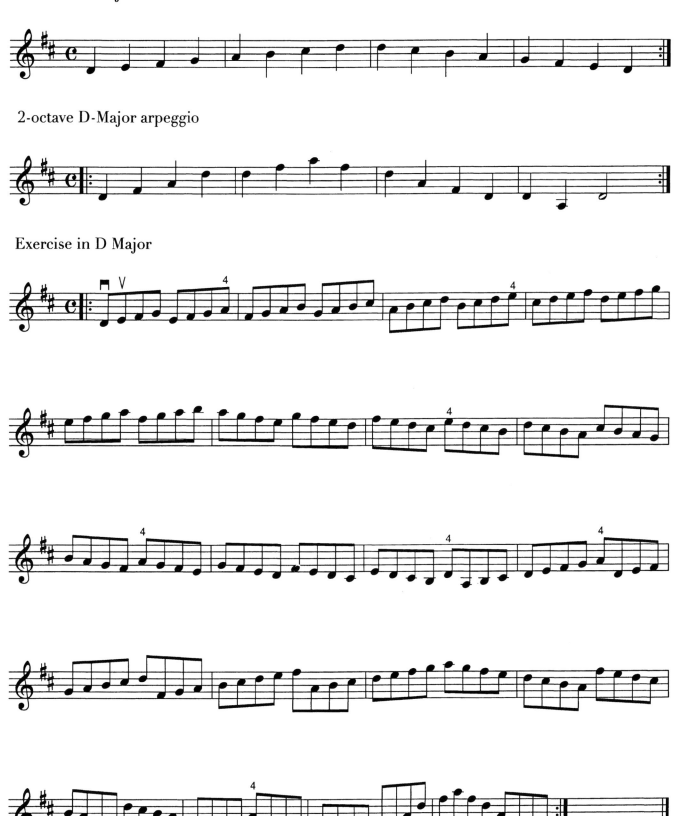

B minor: Scales & Arpeggios

B minor is the relative minor to D Major. While this exercise uses the melodic minor scale, like the previous minor scale exercises, it's important to remember that there are also two other types of minor scales: the "natural minor" scale, played without adding any accidentals, and the "harmonic minor" scale that raises only the 7th tone of the scale and is used when making chords. The melodic minor scale is traditionally used in scale exercises because it is the version you most commonly encounter in single-line music.

2-octave B-minor scale

2-octave B-minor arpeggio

Exercise in B minor

Exercises in D Major & B minor

Exercise 1 in D Major - Odell   Play the dotted eighths with a down-stroke, and the sixteenths with an up-stroke. Remember that the dotted eighths are three times as long as the sixteenths, so be sure to hold them for their full value.

Exercise 2 in B minor - Branzoli   Tremolo under the slur markings in this exercise.

Exercise 3 in B minor - Branzoli Play the eighths down-up, and tremolo the last line.

Exercise 4 in D Major & B minor - von Sponer You'll use a specific picking pattern in this piece, to produce a continuity of sound. It's marked in the first measure and is to be used throughout the exercise.

continue with this picking

A Major: Scales & Arpeggios

The key signature for A Major has 3 sharps: C#, F#, and G#. Sharps are always added to a key signature in the same order, so if you have G# you will also always have C#, which is the second sharp added, and F#, always the first sharp. In key signatures that use sharps, the name of the key is always one note higher than the last sharp. So you know, if the last sharp (the one to the right as you read across) is G#, that you are in the key of A Major.

2-octave A-Major scale

2-octave A-Major arpeggio

Exercise in A Major

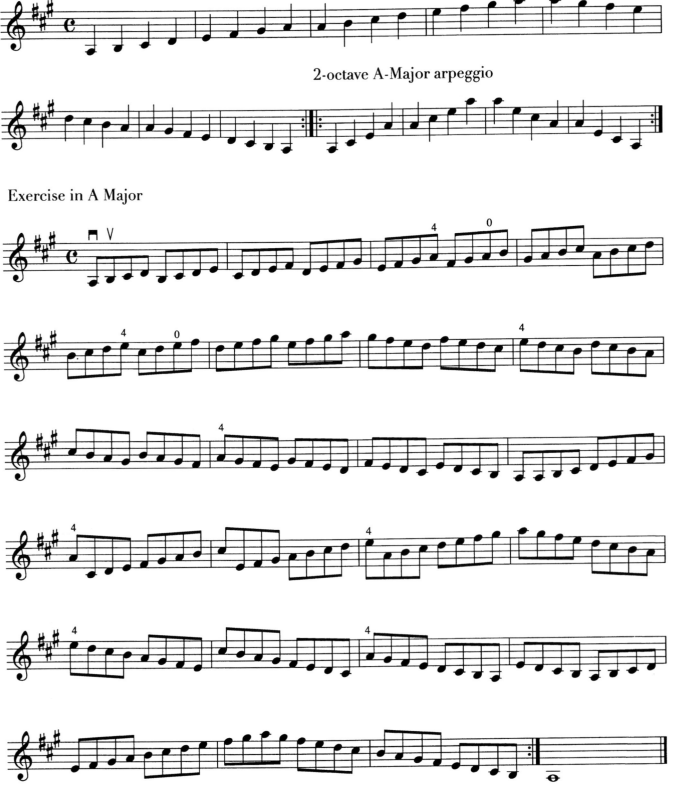

F♯ minor: Scales & Arpeggios

F♯ minor is the relative minor of A Major. Use the 4th finger as indicated, and watch the other fingering carefully. You'll notice that the raised 7th in the scale is an E♯, and E♯ = F. So you'll play the E♯ with your first or second finger on the E string, and then slide your finger up a fret to play the F♯ as well.

1-octave F♯-minor scale

2-octave F♯-minor arpeggio

Exercise in F♯ minor

Exercises in A Major & F# minor

Exercise in A Major - Odell Play eighth notes with down-strokes and sixteenth notes down-up.

Exercise in F# minor - Odell Play the eighth notes with alternating down-up strokes.

Bill Cheatham This traditional fiddle tune in A has lots of versions—try changing it a bit yourself.

E Major: Scales & Arpeggios

The key signature for E Major has 4 sharps, F♯, C♯, G♯, and D♯. Use the 4th finger where indicated. You may want to use it more often to facilitate your picking pattern.

1-octave E-Major scale

2-octave E-Major arpeggio

Exercise in E Major

C♯ minor: Scales & Arpeggios

C♯ minor is the relative minor to E Major. Use the 4th finger where indicated. Raising the 6th and 7th notes to A♯ and B♯ will affect your fingering, so watch the notations. Notice that you will actually be shifting into 2nd position in the 2nd measure of the arpeggio exercise.

2-octave C♯-minor scale

2-octave C♯-minor arpeggio

Exercise in C♯ minor

Exercises in E Major & C♯ minor

Exercise in E Major - Branzoli Use continuous down-up picking in this exercise. Start on a down-stroke following each rest and continue to alternate. Don't start every triplet with a down-stroke as that will interrupt the flow of the line. Remember that you lose the use of your open G and D strings on this exercise because of the sharps in the key signature.

continue with this picking style

56

Adagio in C# minor - Branzoli Be sure to hold each note for its full value and follow the fingerings given.

F Major: Scales & Arpeggios

The key signature for F Major uses one flat, B♭. Use the 4th finger where indicated.

1-octave F-Major scale

2-octave F-Major arpeggio

Exercise in F Major

D minor: Scales & Arpeggios

The key of D minor is the relative minor of F Major, and shares its key signature of one flat. Since the melodic version of the minor scale raises the 6th and 7th tones leading up to the tonic, the D minor scale has one sharp ascending and one flat descending.

1-octave D-minor scale

2-octave D-minor arpeggio

Exercise in D minor

Exercises in F Major & D minor

Both of these exercises double each note played. In the first exercise this is written out. In the second exercise it isn't, to save space. Keep a relaxed wrist and emphasize the forward momentum of the musical line.

Exercise in F Major - Odell

Exercise in D minor - Schloming Play each eighth note as two sixteenth notes. The first two measures are written out; continue this picking throughout the exercise. Pick lightly, and only accent the first note of each measure to create a lovely airy texture.

continue this picking

B♭ Major: Scales & Arpeggios

The key signature for B♭ Major has 2 flats, B♭ and E♭. Use the 4th finger where indicated, and remember that you can't use your open E-string since you have an E♭ in the key signature. The order that flats are added to a key signature is B-E-A-D, and the name of the key is the name of the next-to-last flat.

2-octave B♭-Major scale

2-octave B♭-Major arpeggio

Exercise in B♭ Major

G minor: Scales & Arpeggios

The key of G minor is the relative minor of B♭ Major, and shares its key signature of two flats. The melodic minor scale raises the 6th and 7th tones leading up to the tonic, so the G minor scale has an E♮ and F♯ going up, and an E♭ and F♮ going down.

2-octave G-minor scale

2-octave G-minor arpeggio

Exercise in G minor

Exercises in B♭ Major & G minor

These exercises, in 9/8 and 6/8, work on triple picking patterns. There are two main triple patterns, a straight alternation of down-up strokes, that I call "Bach picking," used starting in measure 8, and the d-u-d / d-u-d pattern known as "jig picking," used at the start of the exercise. A number of other picking patterns are used to facilitate string crossings, including a pattern that starts with a glide, found beginning in measure 13. Each pattern creates a different sound and each has its place in the exercises, so watch and listen for the changes.

Exercise in B♭ Major - Ranieri

64

Exercise in G minor - Branzoli This exercise also changes its picking pattern in a few spots, giving you alternating sections of jig picking and Bach picking. Notice how the sound changes between patterns.

continue jig picking

continue Bach picking

continue jig picking

continue Bach picking

Exercise in B♭ Major - Schloming

E♭ major: Scales & Arpeggios

The key signature for E♭ Major has 3 flats, B♭, E♭, and A♭. In this key we lose the possibility of using the open A and E strings, so you'll be using your 4th finger frequently. If you're tempted to skip this scale, because folk music isn't written with flats, think again. If you ever plan to play with sax or clarinet, or to play the Beethoven "Adagio" for mandolin, or investigate choro or jazz, you'll need this scale. So just do it.

1-octave E♭-Major scale

2-octave E♭-Major arpeggio

Exercise in E♭ Major

C minor: Scales & Arpeggios

C minor is the relative minor of E♭ Major. Because of the raised 6th and 7th tones, the scale has an A♮ and B♮ on the way up and an A♭ and B♭ on the way down. This is the key of the beautiful Beethoven sonatina that you'll find on page 222.

2-octave C-minor scale

2-octave C-minor arpeggio

Exercise in C minor

Exercises in E♭ Major & C minor

Notice that this key signature eliminates the use of the open A and E strings. Play these exercises with alternating down-up strokes on the eighth notes.

Exercise in E♭ Major - Branzoli

Exercise in C minor - Branzoli Tremolo the half notes, or simply hold them for their full value.

Exercise in E♭ Major - Kreutzer Play this piece with straight down-up picking.

Flow Gently Sweet Afton - *traditional Scottish* This piece introduces the "D. S. (Dal Segno) al Fine" marking that indicates you should return to the "Segno" symbol and play until the "Fine" where the piece ends.

A♭ Major: Scales & Arpeggios

The key signature for A♭ major has 4 flats, B♭, E♭, A♭, and D♭. This eliminates the use of three of the open strings, keeping your 4th finger very busy. Although this key isn't used very frequently for mandolin music, it's good to develop a familiarity with it in case you encounter it in your mandolin journeys.

2-octave A♭-Major scale

2-octave A♭-major arpeggio

Exercise in A♭ Major

F minor: Scales & Arpeggios

F minor is the relative minor of Bb Major. Since the 6th and 7th tones are raised a half step in the melodic minor, we lose two flats ascending, and return to 4 flats in the descending mode. Use the 4th finger as indicated.

1-octave F-minor scale

2-octave F-minor arpeggio

Exercise in F minor

Exercises in A♭ Major & F minor

Duet in A♭ - Odell   I'm giving you duets for these exercises in 4 flats, so there'll be another part to remind you of the key signature. The melody is simple and predictable too, so that should help. Tremolo the half notes as marked. You should learn both parts of these duets.

Duet in F minor - Odell Tremolo the dotted quarter and half notes as marked. This exercise goes into 2nd position at places. Be sure to keep your shift finger down on the way up and back so your motor memory will be able to help you keep your place on the fretboard. The grace notes at the end of the second line are to be played quickly before the beat. There are double-stops in the first section of the accompanying part. I haven't given you fingerings this time, so you'll need to figure these out yourself before you begin to play that part.

Playing in Positions

Now that you've learned all the notes on the bottom half of the neck, it's time to tackle the top half. Playing in positions can be disorienting at first. "B" isn't simply a note played by the first finger on the 2nd fret of the A string. It is still the note read on the middle line of the staff, but its position on the fingerboard has become "unstuck" and you can play it in 3 different spots on the neck. Shortly this will seem natural, but be patient while you learn. This is a very important step in your path forward.

Exercise 1 - Play this scale entirely on the G string, using the fingering given.

Exercise 2 - Play this scale entirely on the D string. Notice you use the same frets as you did in Exercise 1.

Exercise 3 - Play this scale entirely on the A string. Again, you are using the same frets.

Exercise 4 - Play this scale entirely on the E string. It's not hard—it's still the same frets as the other three!

Exercise 5 - Now we're going to play a series of notes in two different places on the fretboard. Take your time. Be sure that the notes in the higher position sound the same as the set in 1st position.

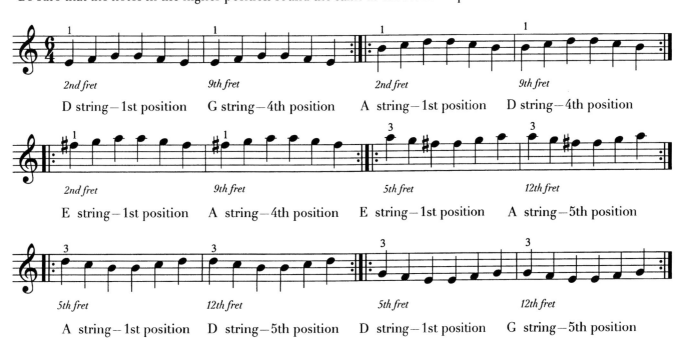

Second Position

This exercise begins in first position and stays there for 16 bars. It then moves to second position and remains there until the last measure. Some fingerings are given to guide you, but remember not to shift back to first position until the last chord. Second position is very useful for playing in the key of C and also for preserving tone color in a melody by adding an extra note while remaining on the same string.

Exercise in Second Position - de Beriot

*This 3-note chord uses a 1st-finger "bar." Flatten your finger to depress both the D string and the A string at the 3rd fret.

Third Position

Remain in third position for this entire exercise. Some fingerings are added as reminders. Keep your first finger down on every string as long as you are playing on that string.

Exercise in Third Position - Wohlfahrt

Exercise in 3rd Position with Open Strings - Wohlfahrt This exercise stays in third position, but incorporates the open D and G strings. Don't add tremolo, just work on finding your notes.

Combining Positions

This exercise works on shifting between the first three positions. Be sure to keep your "shift finger" (the finger you use to shift into the new position) in contact with the fingerboard as you shift, so your hand can learn the distance between positions on the fretboard and remember it accurately.

Exercise in 3 Positions - Pettine

Shifting in Context

In these exercises you'll practice changing positions. When you shift keep your "shift finger" down so you'll learn to move accurately between positions. Don't change positions in these exercises until the fingering indicates that you should shift. You need to learn to be comfortable playing in the higher positions.

Connecting First and Third - Wohlfahrt (fingering by Pettine)

Exercises to Practice Shifting - Pettine
Practice all suggested fingerings and repeat each exercise several times before proceeding to the next one.

Shifting Frequently

This exercise includes frequent shifts of position. It shifts more often than an actual piece would, so don't be dismayed. At first play the exercise slowly using only down-strokes. As you become better able to negotiate the shifts, begin to use down-up strokes on the eighth notes and increase the tempo.

Exercise with Frequent Changes of Position - Pettine

Andante Sostenuto

Giuseppe Branzoli (arr. Mair)

Tremolo quarter notes and above, and play the eighth notes down-stroke. Change positions as the fingering indicates. You'll be shifting into 4th position for the first time in this piece. Observe the phrasing given and, whether you choose to tremolo or not, be sure to phrase over the bar line to keep the piece moving forward.

continue this phrasing

85

Chromatic Scales

Playing chromatic scales on the mandolin involves sliding the left-hand fingers from one fret to the next to play notes on seven consecutive frets with four fingers. Usually in a chromatic run, the right hand is picking a steady stream of eighth or sixteenth notes, so the left-hand finger slides must also match the speed of the pick. It takes practice to master this. Here are some exercises with different fingerings to get you started. Notice the use of an "F double sharp" in the A-string scale, marked with an "**x**" before the note. Remember that a double-sharp raises a note a whole step (two frets) above its natural position.

Chromatic Scale in 1st Position

Chromatic Scale with Shifting on the G string - Pettine   Here's another possible fingering.

Chromatic Scale with Shifting on the D string - Pettine

Chromatic Scale with Shifting on the A string - Pettine   Notice the use of the "F double-sharp."

Chromatic Study - Wohlfahrt   Continue with the fingering pattern notated as long as possible.

87

Moving Scale

This exercise adds the element of shifting to your scale work. Don't be put off by all the sharps—the exercise is simply a 2-octave Major scale that modulates up by a half step each repetition. So you'll begin your moving scale on the open G string. In measure 8 you'll modulate up one fret and play the same scale beginning with G♯. Continue until you are beginning on the 10th fret of the G string. Then work your way back down. This is one exercise that it's probably easier not to read, once you've got the pattern. Remember to start every scale on the G string and keep the fingering exactly the same for each scale.

2-octave G scale

2-octave G♯ scale

1st fret

2-octave A scale

2nd fret

2-octave B♭ scale

3rd fret

2-octave B scale

4th fret

2-octave C scale

5th fret

2-octave C♯ scale

6th fret

88

2-octave D scale

7th fret

2-octave E♭ scale

8th fret

2-octave E scale

9th fret

2-octave F scale

10th fret

Descending scales   You'll now move the scales back down the neck.

9th fret

8th fret

7th fret

6th fret   Continue the 2-octave scales, descending one fret at a time until you reach the G scale.

Three-Octave Arpeggios

Playing arpeggios up the neck is a good way to claim ownership of your fingerboard. In this exercise you'll play the tonic triad and modulate up from one key to the next. I've only included the 8 most-used key signatures here, but you may add others if you like. When you shift up or down keep your shift finger in contact with the fretboard so your fingers will learn the distance of the shift and be more accurate in future.

Chords & the Glide Stroke

All mandolinists should be able to read and play chords on the mandolin. For these exercises, play the arpeggios leading up to the chord with a "glide stroke"—a continuous down-stroke across the strings. Hold all your fingers down until you have played the full chord that follows each arpeggio.

Exercise 1 - Pettine

Exercise 2 - Pettine   Use a glide for the first two eighth notes of each measure.

Exercise 3 - Campagnoli Play these arpeggios and chords as marked. In measure 9 and similar measures, use an up-stroke glide. Use the fingering given or substitute left-hand bars where possible.

Coverdale's Carol

traditional (arr. Mair)

I've arranged this beautiful English carol as a chord solo for mandolin. Notice that the time signature of the piece begins in 5/4 and then alternates with 6/4. There are also several holds at the end of phrases. Play with rubato, tremolo under the slur markings, and observe the dynamics for an effective performance.

 Tr. 10

freely, slowly

C Major: Scales & Arpeggios in 5 positions

It's now time to extend your scale and arpeggio work up the neck. I'll include a few written examples to give you a start, but ideally you should be able to play these without music, so continue to develop this idea in other keys. The suggested fingering is just one way to approach these exercises. Experiment until you find a fingering that works for you.

5-position C-Major scale

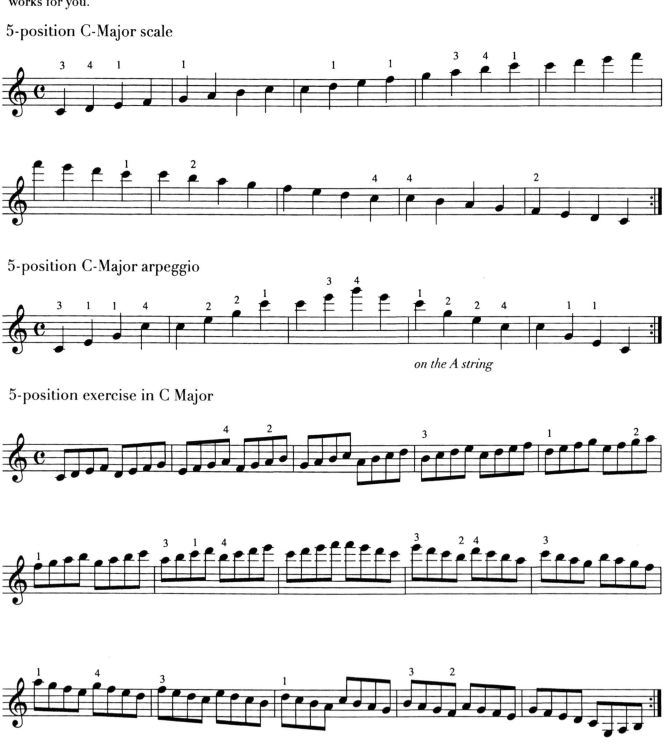

5-position C-Major arpeggio

on the A string

5-position exercise in C Major

94

A minor: Scales & Arpeggios in 5 positions

Watch your fingerings and be sure to keep the minor third (C♮) in the scale. Don't let the scale mistakenly modulate into A Major after the F♯ and G♯ accidentals.

5-position A-minor scale

5-position A-minor arpeggio

5-position exercise in A minor

G-Major: Scales & Arpeggios in 5 positions

Watch the fingering as you proceed. This exercise goes into sixth position to reach the highest G note.

5-position G-Major scale

5 position G major arpeggio

6-position exercise in G Major

E minor: Scales & Arpeggios in 5 positions

Watch your fingerings and be sure to keep the minor third (G♮) in the scale and return the accidentals to their natural state on the descending scale, as marked.

5-position E-minor scale

5-position E-minor arpeggio

5-position exercise in E minor

D Major: Scales & Arpeggios in 5 positions

5th and 6th positions are both very useful in the key of D Major. The arpeggio exercise goes up to the D-Major triad in 6th position. Practice until your hand feels comfortable with the smaller fret spacing at the top of the neck.

5-position D-Major scale

6-position D-Major arpeggio

5-position exercise in D Major

B minor: Scales & Arpeggios in 5 positions

Watch your fingerings and be sure to keep the minor third (D♮) in the scale, and return the altered 6th and 7th notes to their natural positions, as marked.

5-position B-minor scale

5-position B-minor arpeggio

5-position exercise in B minor

F Major: Scales & Arpeggios in 5 positions

The F-Major scale begins nearly an octave up on the mandolin fretboard, so even shifting into 5th position we will only be playing 2 octaves. As always, I encourage you to try alternative fingerings on this and other scales to increase your knowledge of the fingerboard. You should also learn to play your scales by ear.

5-position F-Major scale

5-position F-Major arpeggio

5-position exercise in F Major

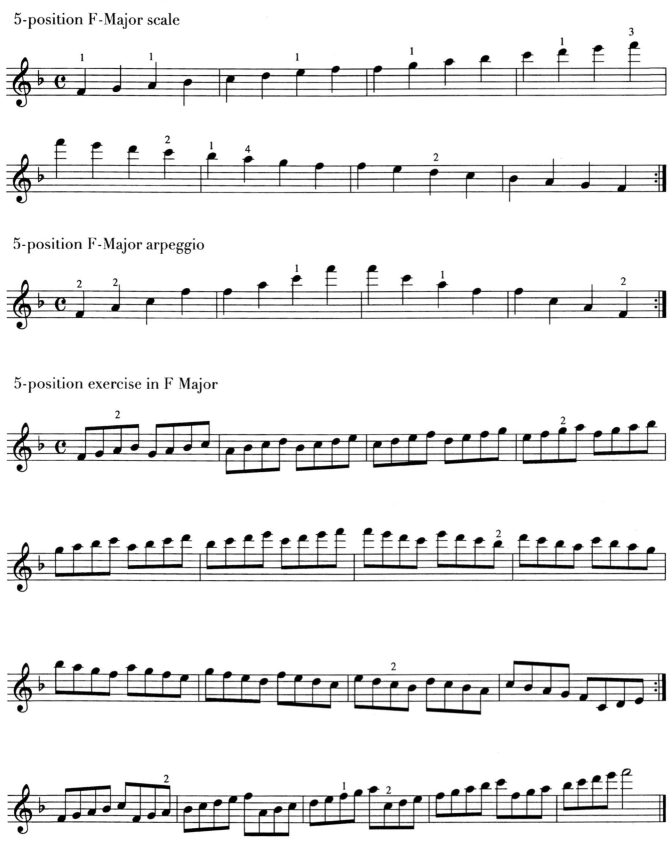

D minor: Scales & Arpeggios in 5 positions

Raising the 6th and 7th tones in this melodic minor scale creates a scale with one sharp ascending and one flat descending. Be sure to keep the D-minor tonality firmly in mind, especially in the descending scale, so you don't inadvertently modulate to a different key.

5-position D-minor scale

6-position D-minor arpeggio

5-position exercise in D minor

Bb Major: Scales & Arpeggios in 5 positions

To avoid using too many ledger lines above the staff, this scale exercise ascends to an "F," rather than a Bb. Don't let that confuse you as you begin your descent. Be sure to maintain the Bb tonality.

5-position Bb-Major scale

5-position Bb-Major arpeggio

5-position exercise in Bb Major

G minor: Scales & Arpeggios in 5 positions

Watch the fingering as you proceed. This scale has B♭ and F♯ ascending, so be careful to stay in the right key.

5-position G-minor scale

5-position G-minor arpeggio

6 -position exercise in G minor

Other Scales in 5 Positions

Here are 5-position scales in some of the other keys. Try to create the accompanying arpeggio exercises yourself.

A-Major scale

F#-minor scale

Eb-Major scale

C-minor scale

E-Major scale

C#-minor scale

The Right Hand

Right-Hand Technique

Your right-hand technique is crucial to your mandolin playing. It is your "voice" on the instrument, creating your musical personality. Besides plucking notes to produce a sound, the right hand also controls dynamics, tone color, and expression. Your pick, your grip on the pick, and the tension in your hand and arm all affect the music you create on your mandolin.

I often have violinists tell me that they could easily play the mandolin, because it has the same strings as the violin. They intimate that they could immediately play mandolin just as well as they play violin. I know from personal experience that this is not the case. I started out as a violinist and when I began to study mandolin it was well over a year before my left hand was doing anything new; violin technique stood me in good stead there. But for that whole first year I was working on my right hand, learning to create a range of sounds, to change tone color, to shape a musical line and, most importantly, to tremolo. I have taught mandolin to violinists, and they soon realize that handling a pick is not as easy as it looks.

Hopefully you're already holding the pick as we described in "Basics" and picking down and up with a relaxed hand. In this section you'll be working on increasingly sophisticated techniques including tremolo, cross-string picking, and arpeggiated glide strokes. So before we begin, I want you to double-check your right-hand technique to clean up any glitches. To develop an efficient, fast right hand, you should avoid unnecessary arm tension and maintain an easy motion in your wrist. I want you to experiment with some "wrong" techniques now, so you'll recognize them before they creep into your playing.

For the first "wrong" technique, hold your pick and mandolin as if you were about to play a note, and squeeze your pick really hard. Notice how your thumb freezes, the top of your wrist locks, and the only way to move your pick up and down is to "push" and "pull" it by moving from the elbow. You do not want this tension in your right-hand technique. Now, as an experiment, hold your pick and place your forearm on a table, palm down, with your wrist bones supported by the edge of the table and your hand extending straight off the edge. To move your hand left and right, you have to "waggle" your hand back and forth, using none of the muscles in your forearm, because they're immobilized by the table. Try "waggling" your wrist very fast. Notice how quickly you lose control of the regularity of motion. You don't want this to be your right-hand technique because it's an inefficient use of the wrist joint.

When you play correctly you'll see, if you look at your wrist, that you're dropping your hand so your pick falls unimpeded through the string and comes to rest on the next string, using the long muscles of the forearm to control your pick motion. Some players worry that this relaxation indicates a "slow" picking technique, and that the "waggle" is faster. That's simply not true. A good tremolo is so fast it obscures the individual notes to create a shapeable melodic line. It is faster than you can count! Increasing speed is easy with this picking style because tension is minimized. When your technique reaches maturity you may actually have to slow your right hand down on difficult single-note runs to match your left-hand speed.

The "Right Hand" section of the book begins with exercises to develop your tremolo, and continues to work on specialized right-hand techniques, like cross-string picking, glides, and reverse picking. Remember that you should be working on these exercises along with those in the Left Hand, Coordination, and Musicianship sections. Your goal is to develop a complete technique and learn to be a musician, not simply a technician.

Tremolo Prep Exercises

To develop a fluid tremolo you need to be comfortable playing continuous even down-up strokes. Here are some exercises to work on right-hand endurance. Keep your right wrist relaxed and pick with a simple drop-lift motion. The down-up picking pattern also creates some cross-string picking in this exercise.

Exercise 1 - Wohlfahrt

Exercise 2 - Pettine   Begin to study this piece at a slow tempo. Your primary objective is to keep your down-up stroke even and relaxed. After you've mastered that at a slow tempo, you'll want to play this exercise and the preceding one several times at the beginning of each practice session, gradually increasing your hand speed as the technique becomes second nature. Use a metronome to help keep your picking even.

108

Developing an Expressive Tremolo

A beautiful tremolo is a joy forever, and a pleasure that is definitely within your reach. Developing a strong tremolo is a slow process though, requiring steady work and patience. Contrary to what you might think, a large flexible pick will not produce a good tremolo. A light- or medium-weight pick does take less effort to move across the strings, but produces a noisy flat sound that will limit your ability to shape an expressive line. Nor can a good tremolo be achieved by filing off the point of your pick. That may keep the pick from getting caught in the strings, but it will also limit your volume and range of tone color.

I'm going to review the criteria for selecting and holding the pick from the "Basics" section to be sure you all arrive at the starting line ready to go. First, check your pick. You need a small heavy one—Fender "small" picks work well and are easy to find. Or if you are more comfortable using a large-size guitar pick, make sure that you have one that is quite heavy, and consider narrowing it slightly at the top to make the shape more oblong and less triangular. Your pick should have a bit of flex—tiny inflexible jazz picks won't work well either—and you need to be sure the pick has a good point. You might even want to file it down some to make it skinnier and pointier. To create a good tone your pick has to be heavy enough to set your strings in motion with enough force to move the body of your instrument, producing a full "body" tone. But it also has to be slightly flexible so it will give a bit on contact with the string, to soften the impact and create a smoother sound. The pick has to be small enough to control without hanging on too tightly, and it has to have a point, to strike the string precisely at one spot to create a clear vibration pattern.

Once you've got the right pick, you need to learn to hold it correctly. With your pick-less right hand in front of you, thumb closest to your face, slowly curl your fingers toward your palm until the first joint of your index finger is running parallel to your thumb, just behind it. Be sure that only the first joint, and not the middle joint is parallel, so the fist is not too tight. Place your pick between your thumb and index finger with the point facing away from your palm. Lower your hand to the mandolin in playing position, wrist slightly arched, and your pick perpendicular to the strings. This is tremolo start-up position.

Hold your pick with just enough tension to keep it in place. Raise your hand by rotating the wrist joint without lifting your forearm, and let the pick fall on the string. Repeat this slowly using down-strokes. Remember to let your hand fall with gravity, it's drop-lift, not push-pull. When you've got the hang of the down-stroke, introduce the up-stroke, trying not to add tension to your wrist. I suggest this daily exercise: Set your metronome at 54–60 and play Exercise 1 on page 23 several times on each string without stopping, consciously releasing tension from your hand on the return to quarter notes each time you repeat. Start slowly, the only requirement is to keep your down-up strokes even and your hand relaxed. Your motor memory, with its natural tendency to speed things up, will take care of the rest. If you devote a few minutes each practice session to establishing consistent picking you'll be well on your way to a great tremolo.

It may seem that I am placing overmuch emphasis on hand position and choice of pick. But time and again I have students come to study with me who are frustrated by their inability to get a good sound out of their instrument or to tremolo well, and they want a quick cure. The right tools and grounding in basic technique are really the only solution. So be sure you have the basics down, that you can pick evenly and quickly, and create a good sound on your instrument. There is no point in trying to move ahead until you can. But while there may be no short-cuts, there is a path that you can easily follow to a great right hand. And once you have achieved an expressive tremolo you will realize that all the attention to detail in the preparatory stage is truly worthwhile.

Tremolo Exercises

Exercise 1 - Branzoli In this exercise tremolo phrases alternate with down-strokes. Be sure to keep a steady beat when you tremolo. Beginners often stop counting when they tremolo and play unevenly, so be sure to avoid that.

Exercise 2 - Branzoli Tremolo half notes and phrases throughout this exercise, breaking your tremolo between slurs as noted.

Valse

Silvio Ranieri (arr. Mair)

Keep your tremolo unbroken under the slur markings, and stop it slightly between slurs. Some of the phrasing may seem counterintuitive at first. For instance, in measures 5 and 6, instead of stopping the tremolo at the end of each measure, I've phrased over the bar line to emphasize the music's forward momentum rather than its repetition. Learning to interpret a musical line, with phrasing and dynamics, is an important step in developing your musicianship, and moving from student to performer.

Tr. 11

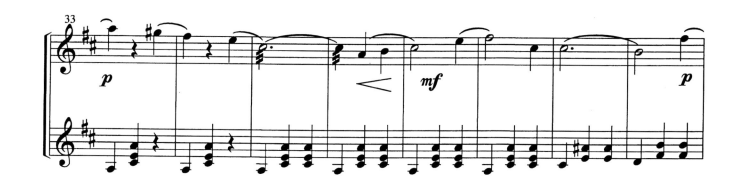

Two Tunes with Tremolo

Star of the County Down - traditional Play this piece slowly and hold your tremolo for the full value of the note. Try to change the dynamics of your tremolo, following the crescendos and decrescendos, by tightening or relaxing your grip on the pick slightly. Be sure to release the tension in your hand after each crescendo. As you grow more familiar with the tune you may want to vary it a bit by adding ornaments, changing your phrasing, or varying the notes you tremolo.

Romance - Pietro Denis Tremolo the phrases under the slurs without breaking between notes. Pause your tremolo slightly between phrases to allow the music to breathe.

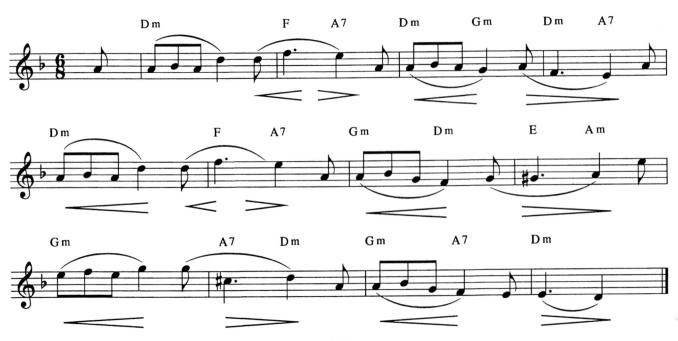

Dark Eyes

traditional (arr. Mair)

This traditional Russian tune uses syncopation and "rubato" (holding the tempo back or pushing it ahead) for expressive purposes. Begin slowly, and tremolo notes under slurs or otherwise marked. Observe the tempo change in measure 17, where you speed up, and measure 25, where you return to the first tempo.

 Tr. 12

Expressive Tremolo

This exercise requires precise counting and a smooth tremolo. The meter of 12/8 is unusual; an eighth note gets a beat and there are 12 to a measure. Since the tempo is slow it may help to count each measure as four groups of three beats each. There are frequent accidentals and a variety of rhythms too. But mostly there is a beautiful melody, and when you have mastered the rhythmic complexities your tremolo should make it sing.

Tremolo Exercise - Pettine

Sheebeg Sheemore - Turlough O'Carolan This lilting Irish waltz benefits from the use of tremolo. As always with tunes in the folk tradition, after you've learned this version feel free to vary the written line as suits your style.

Glide & Tremolo

Giuseppe Pettine

This exercise combines the glide stroke with tremolo. To connect the line smoothly Pettine frequently starts the tremolo on an up-stroke, as indicated. In a glide stroke your pick plays two consecutive notes on two different strings with one continuous motion, creating a legato sound.

continue this picking & tremolo style

Playing Across the Neck

In this exercise we'll focus on learning to play across the neck from one string to the next. The slurred eighth notes are played down-up-down, and the string-jumping eighth notes are played with down-strokes. You'll be using your 4th finger frequently in this exercise.

Exercise in G - Wohlfahrt

continue the same picking

120

Picking Dexterity

Exercise in G - Pettine Keep your picking smooth and even as you move across the strings. Notice when you change strings that your picking pattern allows your pick to move toward the string you'll play next.

Dotted Rhythms

The "dot" in a dotted note makes the note half again as long. A dotted eighth is equal in value to one-and-a-half eighths; a dotted quarter equals one-and-a-half quarter notes. A dotted note is usually paired with a shorter note to fill out the beat: a dotted eighth is paired with a sixteenth; a dotted quarter is paired with an eighth. To play a dotted rhythm correctly, be sure the dotted note of the pair gets 3/4 of the beat, and play the shorter note with a light up-stroke. Don't play lazily—this is an energetic rhythm.

Dotted-note Exercise - David

Concerto in C Major
2nd Movement - Largo

Antonio Vivaldi

Antonio Vivaldi (1678-1741) wrote many concertos in his prolific career, including one for solo mandolin and one for two mandolins. This is the 2nd movement of the solo mandolin concerto. You'll find the music for the 1st and 3rd movements of this concerto in the "Coordination" section of this book. This movement is to be played quite slowly. Be sure to keep the rhythm very strict the first time through each half of the piece or, if you vary at all, hold the dotted sixteenth a bit longer and shorten the 32nd note. For the trilled notes in the last measure of each section, begin a note higher than the written note and alternate those two notes quickly (in measure 6 begin the trilled F on the G and alternate G-F, ending on the F). For the repeat of each section it was customary in the Baroque Era for players to ornament and vary the melody a bit to show their creativity. You can hear how I've done that on the CD that accompanies this book. You'll notice that I've added some notes and varied the rhythm substantially. Try your hand at adding your own ornaments here. We'll learn more about ornaments later in the "Musicianship" section of the method.

Tr. 37

Dotted Rhythms & Tremolo

Adagio cantabile - de Beriot This expressive melody combines the smoothness of tremolo with the brightness of dotted rhythms. Be sure that your sixteenth notes are short and crisp and that they always lead to the next melody note, especially if it's on the other side of a barline. Observe the dynamic markings given, and be sure to play the crescendos and decrescendos for their full dramatic effect on the music. You'll need to establish several distinct dynamic levels in this piece, and for the first time you're asked to differentiate between a "mezzo-forte" and a "mezzo-piano," two different moderate dynamic levels. This will necessarily expand the distance between your loud and soft. Be sure to leave room on the upper end of your dynamics for the dramatic "fortissimo" near the end of the piece.

Syncopation

Syncopation places the accent on an unexpected beat in a measure of music. Sometimes this is done by eliminating the note that falls on the beat, or by using a tie or rest, or by placing a note just ahead of an anticipated accent. These exercises show a variety of right-hand picking techniques used for syncopations.

Down-stroke on the Syncopation - Odell

Tremolo - Odell Tremolo the slurred phrased without a break to create a gentle accent on beat 2.

Down-down-up - Odell This picking pattern clearly accents the syncopation.

Down-tremolo-up - Odell This picking uses the tremolo to accent the syncopation.

Accented off-beat tremolo - Odell The accent and tremolo clearly mark this series of syncopations.

continue the picking pattern

Syncopation & Tremolo

Be sure to count carefully when combining syncopation and tremolo, as it requires precision to play the rhythms as they are written. The accompaniment part in this duet should help keep the rhythm straight. If you find the rhythms confusing, try counting it out without playing. The pick-up and first measure are counted: "3-e-&-uh / 1-& / (2)-& / (3)-&" with the tremolos beginning on the off-beat and extending through the beat.

Syncopated Duet - Odell

Syncopated Tremolo Phrasing - Odell Tremolo this exercise and break your tremolo between phrases to attach the quarter-note runs to the 3-beat note that follows them.

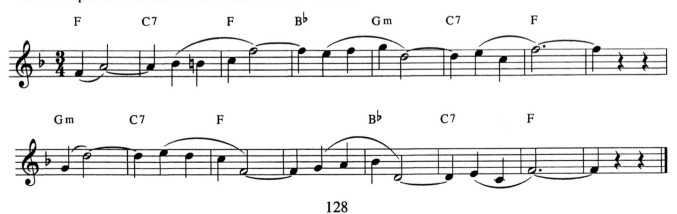

128

A Flor Amorosa

Joaquim Calado (arr. Mair)

Brazilian choro is a style of music that often features bandolim (the Brazilian mandolin) and is characterized by extensive use of syncopation and chromatic runs. This piece was written by one of the 19th-century founders of choro, and will give you a chance to work on syncopation and dotted rhythms.

Tr. 13

Não Se Impressione

Chiquinha Gonzaga (arr. Mair)

We'll end this section on dotted rhythms and syncopation with another 19th-century Brazilian choro, this one written by Chiquinha Gonzaga, the "First Lady" of choro. Her title translates roughly as "Don't Be Impressed with Yourself". Chiquinha was a professional woman composer in an era when that was unusual, and she was one of the first to combine the street idioms and rhythms of Rio with the salon music style imported from Europe. Play this piece at a moderate tempo, and watch the picking given, as it's intended to help express the languid quality of the melody.

 Tr. 14

130

Working on Triplets

One of the most basic and defining elements of music is rhythm. Without beat there is no music, and without differentiation of rhythmic patterns, music would be pretty dull. Rhythm is simple, a given. It's the most basic, easily recognizable element of a musical style, yet in many ways it can also be its most subtle aspect. Sometimes rhythm is straightforward. The difference between a quarter note and an eighth note is clear–the former is twice the length of the latter. Most rhythmic divisions work like this, halving or doubling a note's duration, all in the context of the beat. But in the case of triplets, we enter a new realm of beat sub-division, one that we need to take a second look at.

Triplets present a special challenge. You'll usually encounter them written as three eighth notes slurred together, labeled with a "3," and meant to equally share one quarter-note beat. To easily create a proper triplet, play even down-strokes on your mandolin, and count your strokes "1-and-uh; 2-and-uh;..." True triplets have a legato gliding quality that is lovely to hear. But dividing a beat into three equal parts can be surprisingly difficult to do. Our natural rhythmic tendency is to halve or double a note's value, so triplets are commonly mis-played by dividing the beat into four parts, and playing the three notes as "eighth-sixteenth-sixteenth" rather than three equal units. It's hard to illustrate this subtle variation on paper, but pushing ahead fearlessly, I'll literally use the word "fearlessly" as an example. It's easy to pronounce "fearlessly" as a triplet, while beating an even 1-2-3 /1-2-3. Now, notice how accenting any syllable of the word can change the rhythmic pattern of pronunciation: "FEAR-less-ly" can change the rhythm to "eighth-sixteenth-sixteenth," "fear-less-LY" can become "sixteenth-sixteenth-eighth" and, stretching the point a bit further, "fear-LESS-ly" can sound as "sixteenth-eighth-sixteenth".

Playing triplets correctly is an important skill for every musician to develop. And recognizing when triplets are being played incorrectly is important as well. Triplets are placed in the middle of a run of eighth or sixteenth notes to create a particular sound. You have to know how to recognize and create a triplet before you can discover what that reason is. And your challenge doesn't end there. A good musician needs to be able to play an evenly spaced triplet, and an ensemble musician needs to be able to play a triplet while someone else plays a duplet. This "3-against-2" rhythm is part of many styles of music, from Bach to Brazilian to rap. We're used to hearing it, but it takes practice to play it successfully. It's the little things that set a good player apart from the rest, however, so it's worth taking the time to understand and master the art of the triplet.

There are many triplet picking patterns, each with a different purpose. An unaccented run of triplets might use a straight down-up picking throughout, while an accented triplet pattern, like a jig in 6/8, will work better with a down-up-down pattern for each triplet, or, if there are regular string crossings, a down-down-up pattern with a glide between the first two notes. "Do triplets always have to be played precisely?" you may ask. Of course not. Subtle rhythmic variation is the soul of sophisticated performance and is often used, from Baroque variations to jazz. But, and this is a big distinction, unintentionally inexact rhythm is death to music of any style. You should alter a rhythm only after you have mastered it accurately. Rhythmic variation should be employed for artistic reasons, not because you can't play the rhythm correctly in the first place. And no one will be fooled into thinking the latter is the former. In varying rhythm, you should be 100% aware of what you've done, and be able to undo it any time. So with that distinction in mind, let's begin our study of triplets.

Triplet Exercises

Triplets present a special complication for the right hand because there are many ways to pick them, any one of which may be right for the music you're playing. These four exercises present a variety of picking solutions and you should have them all in your right-hand vocabulary.

Triplets 1 - Christofaro Practice this exercise with a metronome to be sure your triplets are even.

Triplets 2 - Christofaro This exercise uses "jig picking," where each triplet begins with a down-stroke.

Triplets 3 - Odell This exercise uses a strict alternation pattern for picking. I call this style "Bach picking" because it eliminates the accent and focuses on the long line of the musical phrase.

Triplets 4 - Odell This exercise uses a variety of picking styles and introduces the glide as a possibility.

Integrating Triplets with Quarter Notes

Wohlfahrt We will now begin to integrate triplets with quarter notes, so you will be actively subdividing the beat into three as you play. Keep in mind your even triplets from the last four all-triplet exercises, and use a metronome to keep your beats even as well.

135

Playing Three Against Two

Christofaro - This is the final test for your triplets — playing the three notes evenly over two eighth notes. Correctly played, a triplet over eighths sounds fluid and lyrical, but you'll have to resist the pull to "match" the triplet to the eighths by turning it into eighth-sixteenth-sixteenth. You'll also play some two-note triplets, made up of a quarter and an eighth note. The quarter-note gets 2/3 of the beat, and the eighth gets 1/3. Notice how the triplets lead into the next quarter note. Try to arrange your picking to facilitate that.

 Tr. 15

136

Integrating a Variety of Rhythms

Pettine - This exercise will test your ability to keep the "big beat" in your playing. As you move between the various picking patterns we've studied—triplets, dotted rhythms, tied notes, two-note triplets (a quarter note that gets 2/3 of the beat and an eighth note that gets 1/3), and tremolo—be sure to keep the pulse of the music steady, while playing expressively. Working with a metronome will help. I know from teaching experience that the rhythms in measure 4 and measure 22 are especially problematic, so count them out before you begin. Observe the picking and phrasing indicated and use tremolo freely once you've mastered the rhythm.

Adagio molto espressivo

Cross-String Picking

It's important to train your right hand to be able to move quickly and accurately from one string to the next. These five exercises all use one or several repeated notes as an "ostinato" to play the melody against. So each piece actually has two separate lines incorporated into one. Learn to recognize and separate these two elements in your mind, so you'll be able to express the dual nature of the musical line.

Exercise 1 - Wohlfahrt

Exercise 2 - Leone This exercise features a melody on a lower string accompanied by a repeated-note ostinato on an upper string. Hold the melody note—the first note of each sextuplet—so the melody carries through and the connection between the melody notes is apparent. As you progress through the exercise notice how the detached melody notes grow into arpeggios and finally scale passages.

Exercise 3 - Odell Use "reverse picking" (up-down) throughout this exercise.

Exercise 4 - Odell Use down-up picking for this exercise.

Exercise 5 - Leclair You'll use many of the picking techniques you've learned so far in this exercise.

142

Reverse Picking

Sometimes it can be useful to reverse the normal picking pattern when playing constant sixteenth notes with a lot of string crossing. Follow the picking given, and notice the glide strokes used to "reverse" the pattern.

Exercise in C - Kreutzer

Concerto al Unisono op. 6 nr. 3

3rd Movement — Evaristo Felice dall'Abaco

This movement from the concertos of dall'Abaco (1675–1742) incorporates many of the techniques you've studied to this point. Observe the dynamics and change quickly without crescendos or decrescendos as was characteristic in the Baroque Era. Remember to begin your trills on the note above the written note.

Arpeggios Across the Strings

In the Left Hand section of the book you played arpeggios that shift up the neck. In these exercises you'll arpeggiate chords voiced across the strings. The glide technique you'll use falls halfway between striking an un-arpeggiated chord and playing each of the four notes separately. Place your pick on the G string and lead with the weight of your hand, dragging the pick down across all four strings, allowing it to catch briefly on each string in order to separate the notes. To play the up-stroke arpeggio, reverse your hand and lead the pick up from the wrist. Practice this technique on your open strings first.

146

147

Three-String Arpeggios - Pettine
To play arpeggios on three strings instead of four you need an even more precise right-hand picking pattern. Play lightly, and remember to separate each note on the glide strokes. Keep all fingers down for each full arpeggio, and use two-string bars where needed.

148

Coordination Exercises

Coordinating Left & Right

There isn't a musician alive who doesn't want to be able to play his/her instrument faster and cleaner. We admire performers who can run through a passage of fast sixteenth notes seamlessly, focusing us on the music they perform without the slightest fumble to distract our attention. One of the difficult aspects of achieving a clean, clear sound on the mandolin is that tone production relies on the precise coordination of two very different hand motions. The pick, held in the right hand, and any one of four left-hand fingers need to contact the instrument simultaneously in rapid sequence. Coordinating your hands to do this at the rate of 8 times a second (necessary to play sixteenth notes at mm 120) requires honing one's precision.

There are many ways to go about achieving this level of technique. Just playing a lot will increase your speed, as your "motor memory" remembers each action you take and, with repetition, that will decrease the amount of time you need to recall and execute it. This is the reason musicians and athletes practice on a daily basis. But the other aspect of playing fast is accuracy, and that requires a whole different set of drills. Knowing and executing the correct movements precisely on time will determine the cleanness of your technique. Merely increasing your speed won't magically remedy sloppiness.

There are many ways to get your fingers working more efficiently with your pick. Finger alternation exercises on one string or moving across the strings build strength and coordination. You can make these up yourself, as pretty much any combination will do, as long as you work with intention, not randomly. Playing scales and arpeggios daily–long after you have learned the notes–will also help you to increase your speed and accuracy. When I was working to improve my coordination I compiled a series of exercises that I liked, and had already studied, and I would play each one 6, 8, 10 times in a row, before moving on to the next. I would do this for an hour or two daily in an early morning practice session, before beginning to work on repertoire. You can

approach coordination any way that will work for you, but the bottom line is that you have to choose to do something specific; simply playing through current repertoire and learning new pieces isn't a good approach for the long run.

To prepare for the technical situations you will encounter in future musical endeavors, you need a strong grounding in mandolin problem-solving, the kind that comes from working regularly on exercises designed to improve coordination. These pieces need to be long enough for you to develop your stamina too. It doesn't make sense to prepare for a 20-minute sonata performance, or a 45-minute bluegrass set, by working on a series of short 32-bar exercises. Maintaining your skill level for the duration of an entire performance requires you to be in top technical shape, so endurance, as well as coordination, is your goal.

For this section of the book I've combined pieces from early mandolin and violin methods with movements from Baroque concert music to create a series of coordination scenarios for you to explore. The "motor rhythm" of the Baroque is especially good for improving your coordination as the pieces include long unbroken strands of fast notes that test and improve your ability to combine the technique of your left and right hands to create one unified gesture.

Practice these exercises with a metronome, and begin at a slow tempo to avoid making and reinforcing mistakes at the early stages. Maintain a regular down-up picking pattern throughout, except where marked otherwise. As you become familiar with an exercise you may increase your tempo, a little at a time, and begin to repeat pieces two or more times without pause and include several in a practice session. Try to play with the flow of the music, not allowing your technique to break its line. Good coordination is crucial to good, fast playing, but pushing too hard can cause an injury, so be sure to increase your speed conservatively.

Etude No. 3

Samuel Siegel

We'll start with an exercise to get your hands working in synch across the fingerboard. The right hand moves between "Bach picking" (measure 1) and "jig picking" (measure 6) with accidentals added throughout the piece. Begin this exercise at a slow tempo and work on playing the notes cleanly before you increase your speed.

Bringing Your Left Hand Up To Speed

Exercise in G - Wohlfahrt Good coordination requires that your hands be able to change tempos precisely and in unison. In this exercise the first set of sixteenth notes in each measure changes your right-hand speed, and then the second set brings your left hand up to the same tempo. Practice this exercise with a metronome to establish accuracy. You're working with short bursts of speed here, so be sure to relax your hands on the quarter notes, and hold them for their full value. Play lightly.

Exercise in G - Wohlfahrt

153

Left-Hand Finger Placement

This exercise combines scale passages, accidentals, and repeated note alternations, to help you focus on improving the precision of your left-hand finger placement. Begin at a slow tempo and be sure to play cleanly. You may increase the tempo after you have developed accuracy. This exercise introduces much longer coordination passages. Don't move ahead to it until you are ready. You may want to play just half of the exercise at first until you build up your endurance.

Exercise in G - Schloming

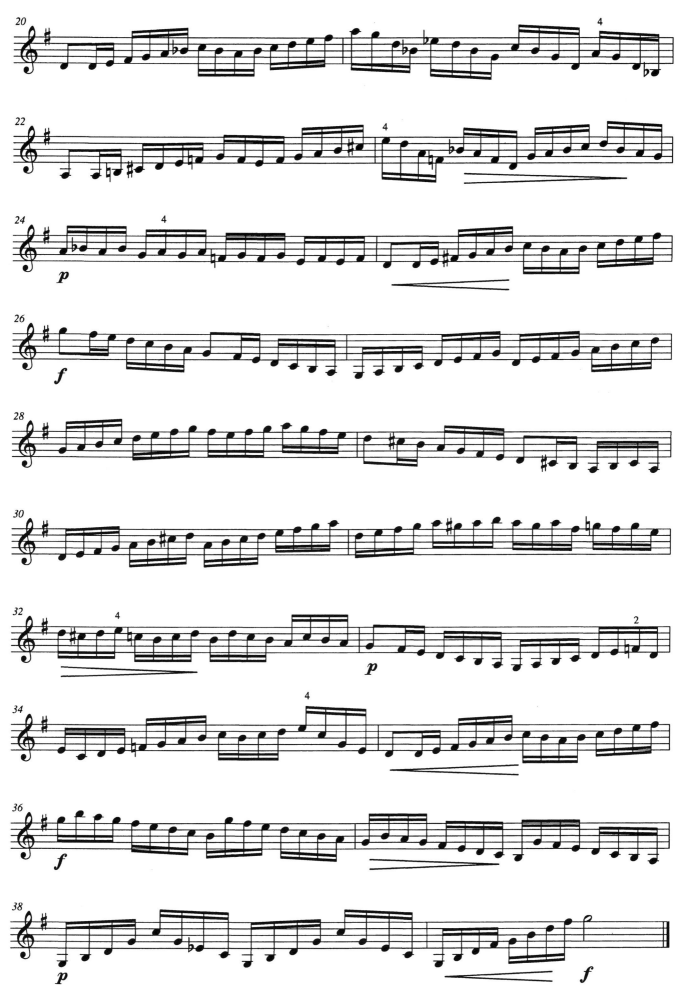

Developing Dexterity

These exercises present complex series of running notes combining arpeggios, sequences (a pattern of notes that repeats as it moves up or down in pitch, as in measures 7–8 on this page) and pedal tones (a repeating bass note interjected into a melodic phrase, as in measures 24–25 on this page). Play these exercises with accuracy, no matter how slowly you may need to play to do so. You want to commit the finger connection to memory correctly.

Exercise 1 - David

Exercise 2 - Corelli

Exercise in Thirds

Kayser - This exercise works to improve your ability to play thirds—notes separated by 3 or 4 frets.

159

Exercise in A Major

Corelli - This lovely exercise is one of my favorites to warm up with before a practice session. Remember to keep the music moving forward by phrasing across the bar line.

Broken Arpeggios

Schloming - Traversing the fingerboard by leaps instead of steps requires a firm knowledge of the fretboard, and finely tuned coordination between your hands. Concentrate on playing cleanly and accurately.

Leaps of an Octave or More

Campagnoli - In this exercise you'll move from one string to the next frequently, often leaping over one or two strings on your way. This will develop your pick coordination in a different way—you'll be moving the pick further between notes and avoiding in-between strings. Resist the impulse to pull your pick out of the way or otherwise manipulate your right hand to accomplish this. In this exercise you're learning to navigate differently, using your forearm, but you should not be changing your basic right-hand position or the way you hold your pick. Play the exercise slowly at first, and use only down-strokes. Keep your right hand relaxed yet controlled and give yourself time to improve your accuracy.

Concerto in C Major
1st Movement - Allegro

Antonio Vivaldi (arr. Mair)

Antonio Vivaldi wrote many concertos in his prolific career, including one in C for solo mandolin and one in G for two mandolins. This movement uses the cross-string picking techniques you've been practicing. You'll also be using the "hammer-on" left-hand technique. In the repeated figure with 32nd notes (the first one is in measure 26) play the first note with a down-stroke, and while that note is ringing hammer your 1st and 2nd fingers down to play the next two notes without using the pick. Beginning in measure 50 you'll use a variant of this, a "pull-off / hammer-on" to achieve the same effect.

Tr. 36

Matching Hand Speed

Meerts - This exercise combines constant right-hand motion with changing speed in the left hand. Keep your picking smooth and fluid as your left hand varies from whole notes to precisely synchronized sixteenth notes. In measures 2, 6 and 18 you see a "measure repeat" symbol, indicating that you should repeat the previous measure In measure 5, the two slashes across the stems of the half notes indicate that they are to be played as sixteenth notes, not tremoloed.

166

String-crossing and Speed-matching

Pettine - Here's another exercise to fine-tune the coordination of your hands when moving across the neck and playing fast repeating passages of sixteenth notes. Move your right hand quickly between strings and hold your fingers down as long as possible, to allow the lower melody notes to ring against the upper repeated notes.

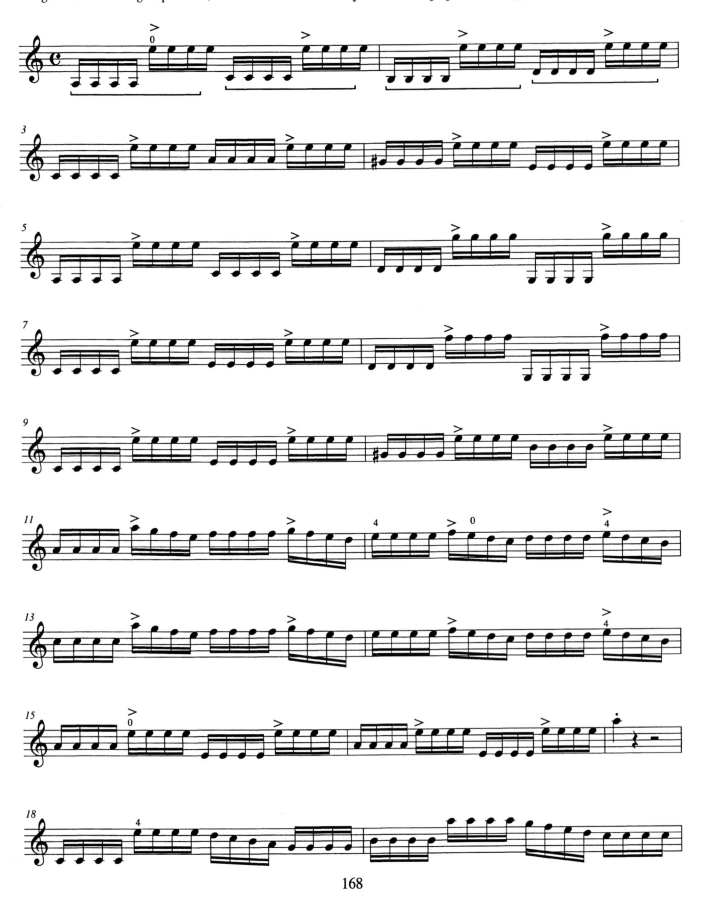

168

169

Concerto in C Major

3rd Movement - Allegro

Antonio Vivaldi (arr. Mair)

This is the third and final movement of Vivaldi's solo mandolin concerto. Follow the picking and fingering given even if it feels awkward at first. It's designed to promote unity of sound through the many sequences.

Tr. 38

170

171

Triplets & Shifting

Kayser - This exercise gives you an opportunity to work on shifting seamlessly in an unbroken sequence of notes. Use an alternating down-up picking pattern throughout, even though there are 9 notes in a measure, to keep the lines fluid and the music moving forward.

172

Shifting Quickly and Often

Kayser - This exercise moves through five positions within the context of an unrelenting stream of sixteenth notes.
Follow the fingering exactly, and don't shift out of a position until the fingering indicates that you should do so.

175

Chromatic Scales & Shifting

Pettine - This exercise continues chromatic scale work up the neck. Watch the fingering carefully and be sure to slide your fingers quickly in the chromatic passages to produce clean-sounding notes. Chromatic scales on the mandolin are one of the biggest challenges for coordinating your left and right hand, and combining them with shifting doubles the difficulty. Practice this exercise slowly at first to solidify the precision of your finger placement before increasing your speed. Tremolo the half notes if you like, or simply hold them for their full time value.

on A-string

Fine

Velocity Study

Pettine - Play this perpetual motion piece with a metronome, and gradually increase your speed as you master the notes. You may need to start by doing half of this exercise and adding segments as your endurance improves. Never play to the point of tension or pain in your left hand. This piece incorporates glide strokes so watch your picking carefully.

Sonatina in C Major

L. V. Beethoven (arr. Mair)

This is one of six pieces Beethoven wrote for mandolin and harpsichord. Manuscripts for only four of these exist today. This Sonatina has been called Beethoven's "best fiddle tune," and with that in mind I've arranged the harpsichord part in lead-sheet format, to make it possible to play with a good guitarist. I added melody notes from the harpsichord right hand in measures 27–30 and 116–119 as the mandolin rests in those measures. Listen to the original version on the book CD to create a convincing realization of the accompaniment part.

Tr. 35

Preparing for Duo Style

"Duo style" is a technique that combines a tremoloed melody with plucked chords. The aim is for the player to sound like two mandolinists by "sneaking" the pick over to the adjacent string or strings to play an accompaniment while appearing to maintain an unbroken tremolo on the melody. Be sure to maintain an even rhythm in the top line of these exercises while playing the lower line.

Exercise 1 - Play slowly at first and concentrate on keeping your notes even.

Exercise 2 - Siegel Keep the top line even, increasing the length of your up-stroke to play the lower notes.

Exercise 3 - Tremolo the whole notes while playing even quarter notes underneath.

Exercise 4 - Siegel Try to keep the tremolo as continuous as possible while changing the lower notes.

Exercise 5 - Strum through the chord and tremolo the top note while sneaking the pick back to grab the next chord. Try to maintain the illusion that the whole note is played with an unbroken tremolo.

Welsh Lullaby (arr. Mair) - This is a beautiful melody that should be played slowly and expressively, using a slight rubato (holding the notes back or pushing them ahead of the beat) to evoke an appropriate tenderness. Tremolo the melody only, but hold the accompaniment notes as long as possible.

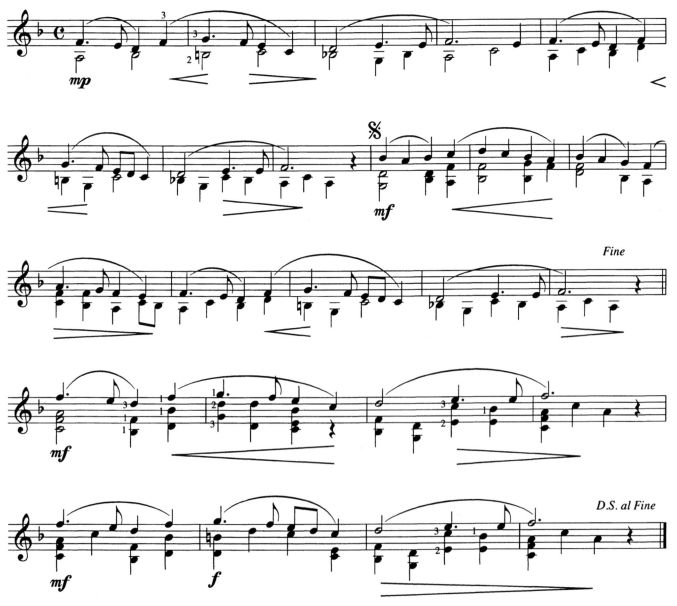

To A Wild Rose

Op. 51, No. 1

Edward MacDowell (arr. Mair)

Play slowly and freely, with rubato and expressive use of your own dynamics. Tremolo notes with stems up, and play the melody as legato as possible. Arpeggiate the accompaniment chords slightly, but don't tremolo them.

with simple tenderness

185

Two by Stephen Foster

Old Folks at Home (arr. Pettine) - Play the melody notes, written with the stems up, with a tremolo, and allow the accompanying chords to ring for their full time value, but don't tremolo them.

Oh! Susanna (arr. Mair) - This is a chord melody solo and meant to sound like a banjo, so strum the chords, but don't tremolo.

Musicianship

Developing Musicianship

A piece of written music, until it's played, is like a beautiful piece of fabric folded on a shelf. It needs an artist to unfold it and arrange its beauty for others to appreciate. As a performer, you are responsible for shaping each piece of music you play. You can create a masterpiece, with the help of a gifted composer, or cut the composition's potential beauty to shreds by your interpretation. Performance is about unlocking potential—yours, your instrument's, and the music's. Beyond learning to play the written notes, you have to consider the shape you, as the performer, can give to a piece of music. Your performance reconstitutes the black dots on the page, and, like a good photographer, you have to find the angle, the lighting, the nuance that will render your particular depiction a work of art, not merely a snapshot. Too often a student thinks the task is complete when the notes are learned. But that, for a performer, is only the beginning. The unfolding of a musical line, the shape of a phrase, the end of a note, these are all aspects you need to consider to create a performance that will inspire.

Performing well requires understanding your music. First, there is the inherent structure of the piece itself. Sonata form, rondo, da capo, through composed—each form must be recognized and acknowledged in the performance. Another important element to consider is your use of dynamics. Usually it's not hard to figure out what you should do. The composer has decided that a particular phrase should be played louder or softer, or that a crescendo or decrescendo is needed, and has written directions that you would be wise to heed. The mandolin is a relatively soft instrument, however, so there is a tendency to play music written "piano" or "mezzo-piano" at a "mezzo-forte" or "forte" level. But you are doing a disservice to the music and your instrument's dynamic range by pushing your soft levels louder. If you can learn to create a solid "piano," not wishy-washy, but gentle and secure in its quietude, you give yourself a broader sonic palette and double your dynamic range. And if you can distinguish noticeably between your "forte" and "fortissimo," you give your instrument the chance to surprise the audience with its power and strength.

You can check how well you are using your instrument's dynamic range by recording your performances and practice sessions and listening back, sheet music in hand. Do you really follow the composer's indicated dynamics, or have you simplified and flattened them out? To establish familiarity with your potential dynamic range, try changing dynamics gradually while practicing exercises, or alternating measures of loud and soft playing, trying to increase the sonic distance between the two. As a performer, it's crucial to your interpretive potential to develop your sonic palette and recognize if you're using it correctly or you'll under-utilize the easiest and most dramatic aspect of interpretation at your disposal.

The style of music you are playing will also have an impact on your interpretation, at least it should. If your 6/8 piece is an Irish jig, a heavy accent on the beat may be just right, but if the gigue was written by Bach, a long unaccented line will serve the music better. In some bluegrass or jazz tunes it may be good performance practice to "swing" a pair of eighth notes to create an unequal long-short rhythm. If you don't play this way you are not observing the established performance practice of the style. But you have to be able to hear when you are doing this, so it doesn't become the only way you can play those eighth notes. Because if your taste changes to include classical music or even Brazilian choro, that interpretation will be stylistically incorrect and your "swing" will be doing a disservice to the music. Classical music itself has conventions that vary by style period. A grace note in the Baroque Era is played quite differently than one in the Romantic Era. And a grace note in the Classical Era, rather than being a quick decoration, actually gets at least half of the main note's beat. A "trill" or "turn" varies not only by style period, but by country. The use of rubato, that can be so delicious in a Romantic-era piece, can utterly destroy the delicate symmetry of music from the Classical Era. Even improvisation has different conventions in jazz or bluegrass, or rock, or choro, or Baroque music.

Varying your phrasing, to allow the music to breathe, is another tool you can employ to shape a successful performance. This concept of phrasing comes naturally when we speak or sing. We accent certain syllables or notes, and arrange our words so we complete a thought or a line before our breath ends. The woodwind and bowed string instruments have physical limitations of phrase length, and figuring out breathing or bowing patterns is an important aspect of working out their musical performance. But the staccato pick-based nature of mandolin technique lacks both inducements to legato connections and specific movements to define the end of a phrase. It is important for you to realize this, and learn how to accentuate your music's natural phrasing. Swelling the dynamics of a phrase, breaking your tremolo between phrases, determining which notes belong together and should be played with the illusion of being in the same breath, are all important aspects of interpretation. And how do you learn phrasing? A good place to start is to simply sing your line and listen to what your voice does naturally. Observe your innate vocal phrasing and try to duplicate that on your instrument. This will give you a basic phrasing template that you can modify as your interpretation changes or becomes more sophisticated.

Another important idea to consider in phrasing is that all notes have an end as well as a beginning. The ending of a note determines whether it is staccato or legato, and whether or not it is connected to the note that follows it. If you cease to listen to a note after you strike it, you run the risk of developing a monotonous detached playing style. Try to exaggerate the differences in the way you end your notes. Hold the fingers of your left hand down as long as possible to create a legato feel, or end your notes abruptly or part-way through their duration to create a dramatic attack or a more subtle semi-detached sound. Notes all have an end, and considering exactly how this will sound is a subtle way of shaping your music.

When you've got these aspects planned, take a look back at the time signature of your piece, to be sure you aren't over-accenting. A measure of 2/4 should have one accent, not two, and a measure of 4/4 should have two accents. A measure of 3/4 has three beats, but a measure of 3/8 has only one. Subdividing your beat unconsciously can lead to over-accenting, which makes your interpretation sound heavier than it should. A light graceful touch is needed to keep the music moving forward in a way that engages the audience and keeps them listening with interest. Look beyond the notes to shape your performance, and you will be rewarded with a whole new sonic experience.

The pieces in this section are intended as examples of different styles, and all have certain lessons of musicianship to impart. To start, follow the phrasing and dynamic markings that I've written in, and you can begin to add your own variations as you gain experience. The wondrous world of musicianship will unlock the artistry of your playing—and taking the time to develop yours will allow the music you play to reach its fullest potential.

Lyrical Duet

Branzoli (arr. Mair) - Tremolo the notes under the slurs and other notes as marked. Keep a light feel in your playing, appropriate to the nature of the piece. Add dynamics to this piece yourself to reinforce its mood.

 Tr. 16

Celeste Aida

Giuseppe Verdi (arr. Mair)

Tremolo all notes within a phrase, breaking your tremolo only between phrases or where marked otherwise. Accompaniment should be a steady "pick-strum-strum" with an eighth-note beat. Play with fluidity, using rubato and swelling the volume of each phrase, generally up past the middle of the phrase and down for about the last half bar. Fade to silence on the final note.

Tr. 17

Duet in G

J. Pleyel (arr. Mair)

Tremolo the quarter notes that are under the slurs, but otherwise, play quarter notes down-stroke and the eighth notes down-up. Play the eighth-note double-stops down-stroke. Arpeggiate the half-note double-stops slightly by playing the bottom note ahead of the beat and tremoloing the top note.

Tr. 18

Remembrances Mazurka

Giuseppe Pettine (arr. Mair)

Tremolo the notes under the slurs and single notes as marked. Be sure to keep your dotted rhythms crisp. Grace notes (small notes with no time value that precede a regular note) are to be played on the beat. Follow the dynamic markings to add contrast to this nostalgic tune from the early 20th century.

Composite Rhythm

Branzoli (arr. Mair)

The two parts in this exercise are playing different rhythms, so players will often change notes at different times. You'll need to learn the composite rhythm of the piece to fit the parts together correctly and stay in tempo. The composite rhythm is the rhythm of the piece itself, a combination of the rhythms of both parts. So the composite rhythm of the first full measure of this piece is 4 quarter notes, even though neither player actually has that rhythm.

Double-Dotting

Giuseppe Pettine

A "double-dot" increases a note's value by 3/4. So a double-dotted quarter note is held for 1 3/4 beats. The composite rhythm in this piece is complex, so count well. When you are sure your counting is correct, add tremolo, as I have done on the book CD. And when you tremolo and still continue to play the rhythm correctly, you'll have reached an important milestone in your quest for a better tremolo.

Tr. 19

Minuetto Pietoso

Leone

Emphasize the long line of the melody by keeping the eighth notes moving forward. Tr. 20

197

Frequent Accidentals & Double-Sharps

Odell (arr. Mair)

This piece is written in the Key of A Major (three sharps) and adds other sharps frequently as accidentals. In measures 19 and 20 you'll find F double-sharp, written as an "**x**" before the note. This indicates that the note is raised a whole step, played a fret higher than an F♯.

 Tr. 21

Tremolo & Rhythmic Precision

Odell - The first part of this piece alternates between tremolo sections and off-beat pairs of eighth notes that must be precisely coordinated with the rhythm of the second part. Be sure to listen and count as you tremolo.

Iara

Anacleto Medeiros (arr. Mair)

This early Brazilian choro by Anacleto Medeiros (1866–1907) may look simple, notewise, but it's an exercise in playing with rubato and ornamentation. Rubato is a slight holding back or pushing ahead of the beat for expressive purposes. It's done within the context of a steady beat pattern, so time has to be readjusted later to compensate. Ornamentation of the melody is typical in choro on the repeat of a section of the piece. I suggest you start by adding "passing tones," notes of the scale that fall between two consecutive notes, and "neighbor tones" notes just above or below the note you're ornamenting. Listen to the version on the CD as an example, but you should ultimately create your own ornamentation.

Tr. 30

Shaping Music with Dynamics

Branzoli (arr. Mair) - Dynamics play an important role in the dramatic impact of a piece of music. Just as you wouldn't play every piece of music at a moderate tempo, you shouldn't play every piece with a monotone dynamic level. Observe the dramatic shifts of volume in this piece, and plan your crescendos and decrescendos to enhance the musical line. Dynamics bring a piece of music to life. Learning to use them wisely is a crucial musicianship skill for any good performer. Tremolo the notes under the slurs and notice how effective a tremolo crescendo can be. Listen to the version of this tune on the CD as a guide, and notice the wide range of dynamics used, but, at the same time, be sure to personalize your interpretation and make this piece your own.

Tr. 22

Habañera from *Carmen*

Georges Bizet (arr. Mair)

This famous aria from the opera *Carmen* is a good piece to develop your expressive playing. Use tremolo and rubato in playing the melody, and vary the dynamics to capture the intense passion of the music.

 Tr. 23

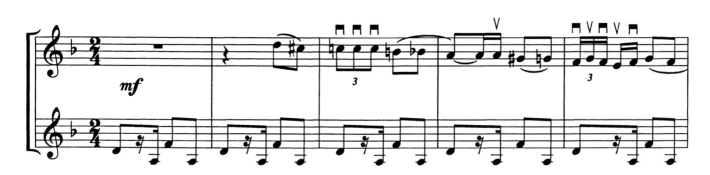

Minuetto Expressiovo

Leone

In this elegant 18th-century piece you'll be playing lines that alternate melody and harmony and parts that switch from melody to accompaniment. There is also frequent use of a pedal tone—a repeated note that grounds the melody—as an accompaniment (measures 5–8) and as part of a single line (measures 11–13). Listen to your part, and the combination of both parts, and decide which notes are important to the forward momentum of the melody, and which are simply part of the musical background. Your understanding of the structure of a piece will inform your performance, and enhance your interpretation. The dynamics are not notated to give you a chance to develop your own. You can hear my ideas on the book CD.

Tr. 24

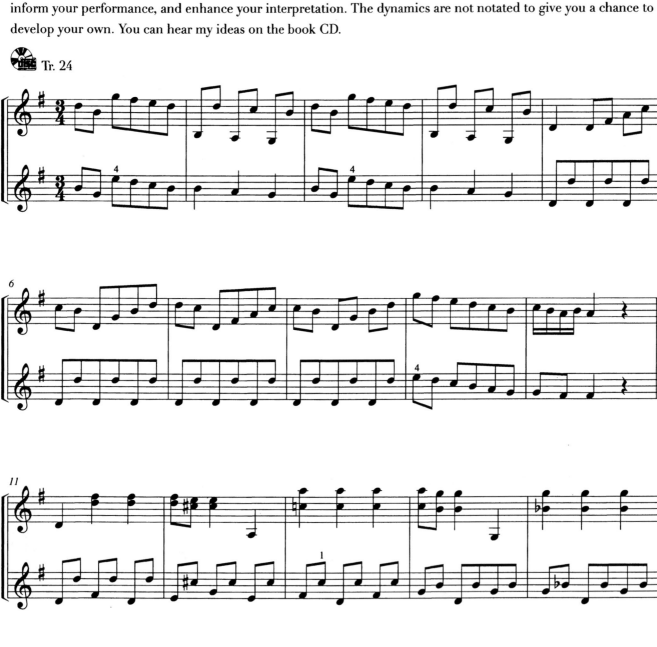

207

Etude in 5/4

Kayser (arr. Mair) - Although most meters have an even number of beats in each measure, you will sometimes encounter odd meters in music. This piece is written in 5/4, and each measure should be played as three beats followed by two beats. The composite rhythm of the piece is complex as well, so count carefully.

 Tr. 25

209

Allegro

Fouchetti (arr. Mair)

It's time for you to approach the issue of musical interpretation on your own. Add dynamics and phrasing to this
exercise, and plan the picking to cross strings efficiently.

211

Invention No. 1

J. S. Bach (arr. Mair)

Bach's two-part inventions for the harpsichord make an excellent introduction to polyphonic music. The slurs here are not used to indicate tremolo—there should be no tremolo in the piece—but instead to indicate how the phrases should carry over to the start of the next beat to keep the momentum of the piece continually moving forward. Ornaments are written in where appropriate. Note the imitative nature of the two voices, and play the piece with those in mind. Again, dynamics are left for you to decide.

Tr. 26

212

Brejeiro

Ernesto Nazareth (arr. Mair)

This lively choro was originally written for piano in 1893. It includes position work, syncopation, double-stops, and double-sharps. Choro's characteristic rhythm—sixteenth-eighth-sixteenth—is similar to North American ragtime of the same era. Play lightly and vary the rhythm a bit on the repeats.

Tr. 31

East of Here

Marilynn Mair

I wrote this mandolin solo on Cape Cod the day after Hurricane Ophelia passed through. It's meant to be interpreted freely with a cheerful jazz swing, so the rhythms are not played exactly as they are written, as is often the case in jazz or folk musc. I've included my recording with bass and percussion on the book CD to give you an idea of how it should sound.

 Tr. 32 © 2005

Gaucho

Chiquinha Gonzaga (arr. Mair)

"Gaucho" (pronounced Gah-oo-shoo) is a maxixe, a lively accented dance that should be played percussively. Utilize interesting dynamics to emphasize the tune's dramatic character.

Tr. 33

Die Zufriedenheit

W. A. Mozart (arr. Mair)

This is one of Mozart's two songs for mandolin and voice. The title translates to "Contentment." I've arranged it for two mandolins with the actual mandolin part on top and the vocal part with added accompaniment on the bottom.

Tr. 27

217

Komm Liebe Zither

W. A. Mozart (arr. Mair)

This is Mozart's other song for voice and mandolin. The title is usually translated "Come Dearest Mandolin," as zither was a nickname for mandolin at the time. As with "Die Zufriedenheit," the piece is arranged for two mandolins with the original mandolin part in the top staff and the original vocal line with added accompaniment in the bottom staff.

Tr. 28

Komm

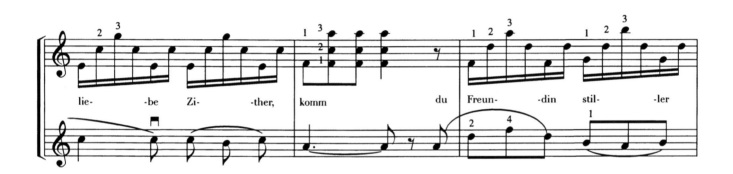

lie- -be Zi- -ther, komm du Freun- -din stil- -ler

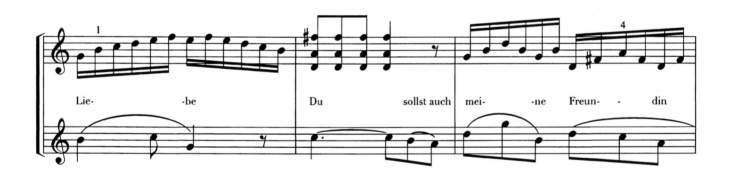

Lie- -be Du sollst auch mei- -ne Freun- - din

sein. Komm

218

dir ver- -trau' ich die ge- -heim- sten mei- -ner

Trie- -be nur dir ver trau ich mei- -ne

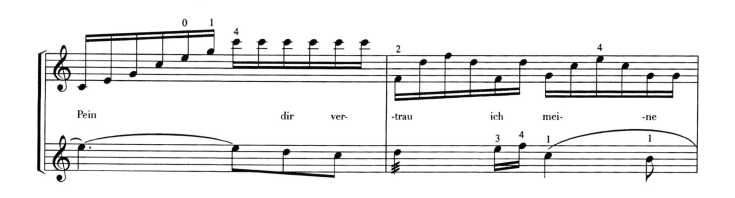

Pein dir ver- -trau ich mei- -ne

Pein.

D.S.

219

Minuet from *Don Giovanni*

W. A. Mozart (arr. Mair)

"Deh vieni alla finestra" (Come to the window) is Mozart's famous serenade aria, written with mandolin accompaniment, from the opera *Don Giovanni*. The original mandolin part is the upper line, and the lower line is the vocal line with notes added at the beginning and the end. Tremolo the melody notes under the slur markings, and keep the feel light.

Tr. 29

Se ne- -ghi a me di

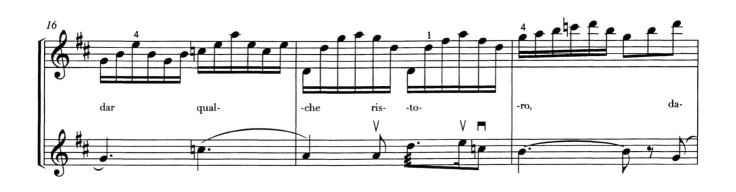

dar qual- -che ris- -to- -ro, da-

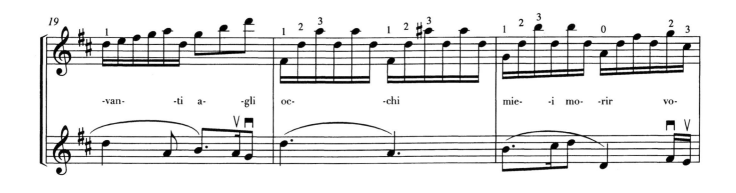

-van- -ti a- -gli oc- -chi mie- -i mo- -rir vo-

-gl-o.

Sonatina in C minor

L. V. Beethoven (arr. Mair)

Beethoven's Sonatina in C minor is a beautiful piece written for the Countess Josephine Clary, a patron and amateur mandolinist. Beethoven dedicated it "pour la belle J par LvB". Play with rubato and expressive dynamics, and follow the phrase markings. You can decide for yourself whether to use tremolo or not—the piece is beautiful either way. Remember not to repeat the first section of the piece on the Da Capo. Keep the melody on the A string where possible, playing up to the octave, to keep the tone color constant.

 Tr. 34

D.C. al Coda

D.C. al Coda

223

CD List:

CD Credits:

Tracks 1–29 were recorded August 30–31, 2005
    at Roger Williams University.
Right channel: Marilynn Mair, mandolin,
    playing the top line of duet exercises.
Left channel: Robert Paul Sullivan, mandolin
    & guitar, playing the lower line of duet
    exercises, and guitar accompaniments.
Engineered by Randy Walters.
Produced by Randy Walters and Marilynn Mair.

Tracks 30– 31 are from Marilynn's CD
    "Nadando em Luz / Swimming in Light"
    (2002)
Engineered by Joe Auger.
Produced by Joe Auger and Marilynn Mair.

Track 30: Marilynn Mair, mandolin;
    Evan Ziporyn, clarinet.

Track 31: Marilynn Mair, mandolin;
    Robert Paul Sullivan, guitar; Nate Davis,
    bass; Brinsley Fair Davis, percussion.

Tracks 32– 33 are from Marilynn's CD
    "Leave Something Unexplained" (2006)
Engineered by Joe Auger.
Produced by Joe Auger and Marilynn Mair.

Track 32: Marilynn Mair, mandolin;
    Robert Mair, bass; Joe Auger, percussion.

Track 33: Marilynn Mair, mandolin;
    Paulo Sa, bandolim; Ellen Santaniello,
    percussion.

Tracks 34–38 are from Marilynn's CD
    "Mandolin in the 18th Century" (2003)
Engineered by Joe Auger.
Produced by Joe Auger and Marilynn Mair.

Tracks 34– 35: Marilynn Mair, mandolin;
    Nancy Nicholson, piano.

Tracks 34–38: Marilynn Mair, mandolin;
    Laura Gulley & Julia McKenzie, violins;
    Noralee Walker, viola; Rob Bethel, cello.